Lost
and
Found

Dogs, Cats, and

Everyday Heroes

at a Country

Animal Shelter

Lost
and
Found

ELIZABETH HESS

Harcourt Brace & Company

NEW YORK   SAN DIEGO   LONDON

**Photo credits: Title spread—© 1998 by Karen
O'Maxfield/Swanstock; p. 1—Valerie Shaff, Photographer;
p. 13—Columbia-Greene Humane Society;
p. 53—Jeffrey Schloss; p. 75—Siobhàn Connally;
p. 105—Camille Praga; p. 136—Equine Advocates, Inc.
1997; p. 164—Beth Linskey; p. 186—Columbia-Greene
Humane Society; p. 209—Cydney H. Cross**

Library of Congress Cataloging in Publication Data
Hess, Elizabeth.
Lost and found: dogs, cats, and everyday heroes at a country
animal shelter/by Elizabeth Hess.—1st ed.
p.   cm.
ISBN 0-15-100337-8
1. Columbia–Greene Humane Society (Columbia County, N.Y.)
2. Animal shelters—New York (State)—Columbia County.
3. Animal welfare—New York (State)—Columbia County.
I. Title.
HV4765.N69H47   1998
636.08'32'0974739—dc21   97-51650

Designed by Lydia D'moch
Printed in the United States of America
First edition
A C E D B

Lost and Found is dedicated
to Kate-Ann Hess Biskind,
my inspiration and co-conspirator.

And, of course, to our pal Snowy.

Don't Anybody Want to Claim Me?

Don't anybody want to claim me?
Don't anybody want me around?
Don't anybody want to name me?
and train me to stand and lie down?

Well, the man, he knows where to find me,
You just ask him for Harry the hound.

Don't anybody want to claim me?
Look I'm down in the lost and found—
'Cause somebody wanted to shame me
and they really went to town:

I requested an ounce of prevention
And it bought me a ride to the pound.

—Timothy S. Mayer

Contents

Acknowledgments

First and foremost, I owe the staff at the Columbia-Greene Humane Society my deepest gratitude for allowing a writer to flourish in their midst. Every person, with no exception, shared his and her experiences and expertise while juggling numerous cats and dogs, not to mention the people accompanying them. I especially want to thank Laura-Ann Cammisa for encouraging me to write about shelter animals. She has had an enormous impact on this book and on my life as a writer. I also want to thank Lee DeLisle for taking me into places where journalists are not ordinarily invited. Both Lee and Laura-Ann have been generous with their considerable knowledge throughout this project. The animals are lucky to have them.

Shelters are fluid places and employees tend to come and go just like the animals. Some of the staff members you will meet in *Lost and Found* are no longer at Columbia-Greene. Others who worked there for varying amounts of time could not be included in this book for reasons of space. I particularly want to note Karen Palchanis, a multitalented "animal person" who was in charge of adoptions when I first arrived; Karen taught me a great deal. Nancy Vallieres and Pam Price did stints in the examination room, always treating me as a welcome visitor. Kate Meehan, trainer and dog lover par excellence, was the first person to show me how to handle resident dogs with love and respect. Adam Holst, a dedicated junior volunteer, can still be found in the kennels when school is out. Sam Shenker spends hours sitting in dog cages, just keeping the animals company, while Judy Shenker labors to find homes for every one of them; Judy is one of the most passionate members of the Columbia-Greene staff. Christine Newman, who runs the Athens facility across the river, transformed an ailing shelter into a thriving one; her sister, Elizabeth Sullivan, is also key to the happiness of animals in Greene County. John Izzo, Lisa Clevenger, and Lisa Coster would have been in this book had I had the pleasure of working with them earlier on in this project. Ron Perez, the rainmaker, has just arrived in the nick of time to run the show and raise some badly needed funds. I know he'll succeed.

My colleagues on the board of directors—Darryll Berman, James Carlucci, Nancy Gordon, Peter Hogan, Charlene Marchand, Gisela Marian, Jonathan Nichols, Chicken Rathbun, Dave Robinson, Scott Shallo, and Michael Wilson—hold the fate of this little shelter in their hands. I hope this book will live up to their expectations.

I also want to thank Dr. Susan M. Tanner, who not only made sure I accurately understood distinctions between hooks and pins, among other worms, but honestly shared her thoughts on a range of issues, including the complex social relations between veterinarians and shelter workers. Others who made vital contributions to this book include photographers Valerie Shaff, Siobhàn Connally, and Cydney Cross.

Making a decision to write a book is not easy. *Lost and Found* might have remained a "crazy idea" had my own family not insisted that I spread my wings and take a sabbatical from the *Village Voice.* Thanks go to both my sister, Lindy Hess, a veteran publishing expert, and my comrade, Virginia Reath, for insisting that I explore new territory beyond the art world. Beth Rashbaum, my personal adviser, led me to my agent, Sarah Lazin, who has consistently offered apt advice and friendship. Sarah championed this book right away and introduced me to the ideal editor. Jane Isay is, quite simply, exceptional. She sorted through my thoughts and my drafts with infinite patience and gentle authority. Jane never lost perspective on even the most difficult material in this book. Her assistant, Lorie Stoopack, graciously paved all the roads that led to a concrete publication date.

The first time I walked into Jane Isay's office and saw a framed picture of Herbie, a dashing Wheaten terrier, on her desk, I knew this book was home. Thank you, Herbie, for having been such a good boy that Jane developed more than a passing interest in the welfare of all animals.

Elizabeth Hess

Peter Biskind, my husband, encouraged me to write this book from day one. His enthusiasm made the difference. Peter not only listened to countless animal stories but remained calm on (most of) those occasions when I arrived home with a four-legged guest. Despite the attendant agonies of two writers living under one roof, Peter remains my most critical reader and counterpart. Thank you, Peter.

In the following book, the names of some people and the biographical details about their lives have been changed in order to protect their anonymity. Certain events have also been combined or relocated.

Snowy

Introduction

HUMANE SOCIETY ROAD is just north of Hudson, New York, off Route 66. It's a narrow road with acres of pasture on either side that dead-ends into a large, run-down dairy farm. In the fall, the hay is baled into immense cylinders that are eventually fed to the cows; if there's extra, it's sold off to other farmers. Wild turkeys, usually two adults with a trail of little ones scurrying behind them, are a common sight in the fields; people stop their cars to watch these large comical birds or to see the tail end of a deer disappearing into the woods. For most of the year, the landscape looks as pastoral as an illustration from the *Farmer's Almanac*, yet civilization—Wal-Mart, no less—is just over the hill.

This book is about four acres halfway up the road, where you'll find a series of ramshackle buildings and a shabby trailer, surrounded by a few chickens and a couple of contented cats. As you approach the parking area, a cacophony of barks grows louder and louder, until it becomes a mournful barrage of howls and cries. I will soon discover that it takes only a short time before the human ear can transform these animal communications into white noise. Welcome to the Columbia-Greene Humane Society.

Animal shelters are the kind of facilities that most people imagine with dread. They conjure up an image of a dingy prison with hundreds of animals pacing in circles or hurling themselves against the doors of their tiny cages, desperate for a friendly pat on the head. "I just can't go inside those places," one friend said to me. "I'd want to take them all home." Instead, people go to breeders or malls to get their pets, buying into the assumption that purebreds are better animals. But this is an illusion. The majority of pet-store dogs start off life in puppy mills, squalid kennels where dogs are inbred, undernourished, and sold for whatever price the market will bear.

According to the Humane Society of the United States (HSUS), up to 25 percent of the dogs and cats who end up in shelters are purebreds, while the rest are garden-variety shepherd and Labrador mixes. These dogs do not come from puppy mills. Millions of them are born every year in backyards, streets, attics, and basements. They are the products of one-of-a-kind litters, the result of spontaneous breeding among all kinds of dogs. "Mutts," as they are colloquially known, are the interracial offspring of pure lineages. They have no official name, no breed or identity that can be linked to ancient ancestry. They have no status in the dog world, an elite club where the stakes are high and traditions go all the way back to Victorian England. The low prestige of mixed breeds, of course, makes the purebreds look even more aristocratic.

Ironically, if there were prestigious shows and awards for mutts, they'd be just as valuable and similarly exploited; puppy mills would spring up specializing in inventive crossbreeds, like the horticultural industry. Right now, these dogs aren't pricey enough to enter the consumer market. The assumption people make is that mixed breeds are in the pound because there's something inherently wrong with them. This assumption is false. Consumers simply want purebred dogs. And there's a thriving pet industry ready and willing to provide them.

Shelters, which operate outside the parameters of the consumer market, are competitive with the pet industry in every way but price. Many, just like the Columbia-Greene Humane Society, offer a wider variety of dogs and cats than most pet stores or commercial kennels. But there's one big catch. Shelters, unlike pet stores, reserve the right to refuse people the animals they desire. They do not sell animals. They adopt them out to good homes.

My hope is that this book will turn the most common myths about shelter animals inside out. When I first learned the disturbing fact that every year almost 20 million animals end up at shelters across the country, I thought it was just propaganda put out by the animal liberation front. Most people I know love their pets. But as I began to spend some time at the Columbia-Greene Humane Society, a number of my own illusions were shattered. Many of my own friends have given up animals for one reason or another. We all have. Animals get lost or become inconvenient when our lives change. If we are often unable to guarantee the future of our loved ones, how can we do it for our animals?

I have always had a fondness for dogs and rarely lived without the company of one. I grew up in New York City with a series of purebreds and mixed breeds. My first dog was a Pembroke Welsh corgi whom my parents purchased from a breeder. Years later, my mother impulsively brought home a handsome miniature schnauzer from Gimbel's department store. But my first true love was a black-and-white hound mix from the Bide-A-Wee animal shelter. She's the one who got me hooked on shelter dogs.

Most of the people I know have had the courage to go to a shelter in search of a best friend. And they always go back for more. Saving a dog or cat is one of life's greatest pleasures. I went to the Columbia-Greene Humane Society in response to a picture in a local newspaper of a longhaired terrier mix named Snowflake who needed a home. The occasion was my daughter Kate's eighth birthday. She had been begging for a dog for about three years. I held off as long as I could.

The moment I set foot in this shelter, I felt a strange and unexpected tug. I found myself experiencing a puzzling, almost magnetic, attraction to this decrepit little facility. I had been to shelters before, but there was something about my experience this time around that was different, more intense. It was as if I had stumbled into another world, a foreign country. I suddenly realized that shelters were emergency rooms for all kinds of animals who had slipped through the cracks of their owners' lives. This facility, isolated like an island in an ocean of farmland, was a demilitarized zone on the frontlines of a war where the animals were suffering the consequences of human failures. The place was a microcosm of incontestable social ailments.

There was also something else going on in this little shelter. The degree of compassion between staff members and animals was extreme. It was as if the staff was trying to compensate for all the abuse these animals might have witnessed in their previous homes. The animals actually came first—before the human beings. Initially, I found the passion with which the shelter employees approached their mission to be excessive, at times ridiculous. In many discussions, they defended the animals and I ended up defending the people. But over time, I found myself absorbing their attitudes and growing more and more sympathetic to their insistence on protecting the dogs and cats. After three years of volunteering my time, my whole perspective on animals and their meaning in our lives has changed. This is how it all began.

As I was walking through the kennel for the first time, a starving miniature donkey, too weak to stand up, was carried in by a man who had found her lying in a field near the road. I wish I had taken a photograph of this man cradling the animal in his arms as if she were human. I followed them to the barn, where he gently put the donkey down on a soft bed of cedar shavings. There were two old goats and a bunch of rabbits already in residence also watching this scene.

I was stunned to see how much concern I felt for a donkey whom I had never laid eyes on before. It was as if I were somehow complicit in causing her misery. Emily, as she was called at the shelter, led me to consider the precise circumstances that lead people to allow their animals to fall from grace into this humane, but frequently fatal, abyss.

A few key questions about the donkey were raised right away: Was it possible to find out who was responsible for this animal's suffering? Was there a decent home available? Would it be kinder promptly to put the old donkey out of her misery? In the half hour that it took various staff members to make the donkey comfortable and begin to assess her condition, I witnessed an impassioned process in which a life-and-death decision was made as routinely as a pot of coffee.

Most shelters automatically euthanize any animal who arrives in serious need of medical attention. Animals are not people, and the logic behind a process that selects one to be terminated and another to survive is complex and difficult to comprehend from a distance. It is a logic deeply rooted in our attitudes about adoption, euthanasia, spaying and neutering, and breeding. These issues affect both people and animals. But we identify so much with animals that it is sometimes difficult to separate our feelings about them from our feelings about ourselves.

The donkey, I am happy to report, was soon on her feet again. She was nursed back to health and placed on a farm with a number of retired horses. For reasons I still don't fully comprehend, I was thrilled by the simple fact of her survival. Emily led me to learn more about other stray animals who were left to fend for themselves. As I did, I soon realized that she was one of the lucky ones; her life could have just as easily been terminated had a number of factors at the shelter been different that day.

In order to write this book, I had to work out my own feelings about euthanasia. I had to chip through layers of my own denial to face the bedrock reality of every shelter: killing animals. Is it purely a moral issue of right or wrong? Are there practical considerations that supersede ethical ones? Is it possible to embrace euthanasia for animals but not for human beings? I found myself thinking about many issues—birth control, abortion, assisted suicide—that are also critical to how people live and die.

I began to visit different shelters, sanctuaries, and animal-control facilities. Some shelters don't euthanize any animals; others have very low euthanasia rates; one puts down two out of every three cats during the summer months. It is raining cats and dogs all over the country, and the majority of these creatures are not getting adopted.

As *Lost and Found* will demonstrate, my mind has taken many turns on all these agonizing issues. It's easy to understand the logic behind euthanizing sick or aggressive animals. The hard question is what should be done with the healthy four-legged dogs and cats whom no one wants to bring home? There are millions of them—the majority are under two years old—waiting in shelters across the country, and they are potentially stellar pets. Ultimately, I believe that no animal deserves to sit in a cage and suffer; death is the more humane alternative. But euthanizing the bulk of them, which is what's happening right now, is no more than an unpopular and temporary solution to a population crisis that most people don't even know exists. Some shelters are starting to refuse to euthanize animals, farming the job out to other facilities. But until we can prevent animals from being born, one animal-control agency or another will continue to be responsible for their routine destruction.

It's odd for a New York City arts journalist to have some sort of epiphany about life and death at a rural animal shelter. Yet I couldn't shake the image in my mind of the animals and their caretakers in this hidden pocket of Columbia County. I realized that every one of the dogs, cats, or donkeys who ended up at this place—which is either their last stop or the first on the road to a new life—was a story to follow. And that these stories were about the social conditions of life in America, where survival for people, as well as their animals, is tenuous.

In 1994, when my daughter was ten (Snowflake had become Snowy, gratis *Tintin*), she begged me to sign her up for a junior volunteer program at the shelter. Somehow, when I brought Kate in, Laura-Ann Cammisa, the executive director, managed to get us both involved in the place. I began by computerizing some materials for the shelter and ended up on the board of directors, feeling the burden of responsibility for every animal who came through. I learned about the business of sheltering animals at board meetings, but the life lessons were taught in the kennels and cat rooms, and by accompanying animal-cruelty investigators on their daily rounds.

I became a witness to a number of dramatic scenes involving a range of animals and people. As a volunteer, I began to understand the predictably unpredictable flow of events at the shelter. Often all I had to do to find the eye of the storm was simply be there. My only lifeboat, on many occasions, was my notebook; I found salvation in the act of taking notes and asking questions. The shelter staff and the people surrendering their animals had so many stories to tell that I discovered a natural role as their oral historian.

My earliest journals are filled with dramas and traumas as I watched animals and people go through painful separations or come together and fall in love. The shelter took me on an emotional roller-coaster ride, complete with exhilarating heights and treacherous curves. I have tried to accurately re-create this experience in *Lost and Found*. But I have also tried to leave the carnival behind and make some sense out of the spectacle.

This book could have been written in any town or city across the country. Animals, and people who care about them, are everywhere. In a sense, I fell into this particular community because it is in my own backyard. But after doing some initial research on other potential locations for *Lost and Found*, I realized that the Columbia-Greene Humane Society is different precisely because the animals come first. Each stray is immediately given a name, toys, a blanket, and appropriate food, depending on the animal's age and condition. Every dog gets a daily walk on a leash and play time in an outdoor pen. The cats are bathed and pampered. Even their nails are clipped.

This place is as good as it gets for homeless animals, yet Columbia-Greene has no money, and its tiny staff struggles constantly just to keep the doors open and the animals alive. The modest scale and the barely manageable volume of new arrivals (about five thousand a year) made it possible for me to know each and every dog and cat at any given time. This was the greatest pleasure in writing this book. The greatest sadness was that I also knew the ones who didn't make it out.

Over the past few years, I have met thousands of faithful dogs and countless exceptional cats, not to mention their dedicated—frequently obsessed—caretakers. I agonized over taking dozens of them home. Instead, I wrote their stories. You are about to meet Grace, Nevada, Bandit, Zack, Catskill, China, Grover, Pip, and the rest of the gang at the Columbia-Greene Humane Society. You will also meet the people who love them and leave them, and those who spend their lives caring for them. Animals attract all kinds of humans.

Grace, one of the mascot cats

ONE

Shelter Shock

THE CRAMPED OFFICE of the Columbia-Greene Humane Society is covered with cat hair. There are files, folders, messages written on scraps of paper, copies of forms, dog biscuits, and cat toys chaotically scattered all over the place. Hand-painted wooden silhouettes of cats frolic around the walls, carelessly suggesting that life is one big playground. A two-way radio, which looks like it barely survived World War II, sits on a desk near an antiquated answering machine. The place is momentarily quiet. The only noise comes from a standing fan in the corner, as it circulates the sticky summer air as well as several large tufts of cat hair. Grace, a slender calico who is a full-time resident here, is curled up in a ball on the copy machine. Pebbles, a gray-and-white longhair with a bushy striped tail and a mask across her face, has just slipped out the door for her morning stroll. These two cats run the front office.

Peace and quiet are rare commodities at Columbia-Greene. At eight in the morning, when the doors are not yet open, there is a sense of calm before the usual run of emergencies. The dog kennels are in the process of being scrubbed in a routine and laborious procedure that begins each day, seven days a week. Laura-Ann Cammisa, the director, is straightening up, annoyed at the mess that has been left from the previous evening. Smells of bleach and dog food mingle in the air.

When I first met Laura-Ann three years ago in the month of August, I was applying for a longhaired terrier mix who had been in the facility for almost two weeks. The dog, a shaggy, bereft creature as cute as could be, was to be a gift for my daughter. I was immediately informed that "live surprises" were a bad idea; I agreed to bring my daughter and husband to meet the dog. My next hurdle was a three-page application that asked a number of detailed questions about my attitude toward animals and required three personal references. The shelter also wanted authorization to phone my veterinarian to find out if I had consistently cared for my previous pets. These people were being careful—very careful. I had to convince them that I was capable of taking care of this dog.

In the beginning, I thought Cammisa was a little excessive. I wasn't exactly put off by the adoption process, but I was amazed by the thoroughness of the shelter's efforts to check on the stability of my lifestyle. The director even phoned the head of the tenants' association in my building in New York City when my landlord could not be reached (then or ever) and asked him if we were good neighbors. From Cammisa's point of view, my daughter was a little young to be getting a dog. Moreover, since I was not a full-time resident of Columbia County, Snowy would be commuting back and forth between the country and the city. I promised I wouldn't let the dog drive. Cammisa didn't laugh.

Weekenders, or "212's" as we are commonly called, are as prevalent as mosquitoes in the Hudson River Valley, only a few hours north of New York City, and about as welcome, so far as some locals are concerned. Laura-Ann is not fond of commuters, despite the fact that she used to be one herself. When I first began volunteering at the shelter, I suggested to her that I might change her poor opinion of New Yorkers. She shot me a skeptical look. "Give it a few months and you'll see why I gave you a hard time with Snowy," she said, smirking. "The weekenders will begin abandoning their animals at the end of August, before they head back for the winter." I found this hard to believe. I had a lot to learn.

Laura-Ann Cammisa is not exactly what she appears. She is certainly not the kind of person one expects to meet in an animal shelter. This morning she is wearing a vintage Laura Ashley dress that ends at her calves and a white cardigan sweater that is covered with tiny white beads. A pair of plastic basset hounds dangles from her ears. Her waist-length hair falls down her back in perfect ringlets that look as if she slept all night in rollers. (She did.) With the exception of the dog earrings, Cammisa looks like she's dressed for lunch at the country club rather than a day of holding, chasing, or just hugging a wide variety of homeless animals. No one would ever guess that this prim, delicate woman is an unrelenting defender of animals.

Laura-Ann switches off the answering machine in the office. The first call of the day comes through like a bullet. She grabs the phone with a crisp gesture before it rings twice. It is a woman who lost her dog three days ago and has finally realized that Nevada is not coming home. The dog, as it turns out, has been a guest at the shelter for two days. He's the color of ripe cantaloupe and almost as big as a Saint Bernard; a dark blue tongue hangs out of his mouth. The woman tells the director he's a purebred golden retriever purchased from a breeder for five hundred dollars.

When Laura-Ann reveals that Nevada is present and accounted for, the woman does not seem pleased. Their conversation starts to get heated as they spar back and forth about the shelter's procedures for releasing the dog. The director listens patiently to the woman's protests and asks her to wait a moment. Then she puts the caller on hold while she explains the situation to me, part of my training as a volunteer.

"The woman is demanding her dog back—right away," Cammisa begins. "But there's a problem. She doesn't want to pay the required fees to the shelter, and she doesn't feel like getting the dog a rabies shot and then a license, which are required by state law." The director has a knowing look on her face. "This is what we get all the time instead of 'Thanks for taking care of my dog.'"

Laura-Ann gets back on the phone and explains in an official tone that the shelter is legally obligated to follow certain protocol before releasing stray dogs to their rightful owners. The state requires verification of a license and a minimum impoundment fee. (A rabies vaccination is a prerequisite for a license.) But the woman could care less about these details. "I just want my dog!" she shouts into the phone.

Laura-Ann removes the receiver from her ear as the woman continues to blast her. "If you want your dog back," the director says sternly, "you have to pay ten dollars for a rabies shot, get an up-to-date license from a town clerk, and pay a ten-dollar impoundment fee. There's an additional ten-dollar charge if I have to transport your dog to a veterinarian's office for the shot. You have two more days to comply, or Nevada will be put up for adoption." Then, in a more conciliatory tone, she adds, "Why don't you start the process by coming in to identify the dog?" The woman reluctantly agrees, but doesn't know when she will be able to get to the shelter. Then she hangs up.

Laura-Ann is steaming. "This woman is looking for an excuse to get rid of her dog. So she's going to blame us for holding him and charging fees, as if we're purposely making it difficult for her to get him back. I guarantee you, if I give her a graceful way out, she will allow us to keep him and put the dog up for adoption. She doesn't want him."

Cammisa turns out to be absolutely right.

I quickly learn the state laws that govern most shelter policies. Stray animals in New York must be held for five days. After their stray time is up, they can either be put up for adoption or euthanized, at the shelter's discretion. The animals go through an evaluation process that determines which road they take. The only exception to the five-day rule is New York City where, as a result of an inordinately high volume of animals, strays are held for only two days. But stray time, whether two days or five, is appallingly short. Owners attempting to find lost pets must move quickly. Those who wait a week, hoping their dogs or cats will come home, often find out they have been put to sleep, a popular euphemism for euthanasia. Small newspapers across the country are filled with poignant stories about angry pet owners who lose their animals to overburdened shelters simply because they did not get to a facility in time.

The oddest thing about this situation is that no one is searching for most of the strays. When I first go through the dog kennels and cat rooms, I cannot comprehend why the owners of all these lost animals have failed to locate them. It's no secret that strays frequently end up at the pound. When I begin to read through shelter files and track specific animals over time, it turns out that many of them have had numerous stray and owned chapters of their lives, passing from one set of hands to another. The animals either disappear or are given away in a vicious circle that frequently leads them to a shelter. The lucky ones make it back out again into long-term homes.

Assessing a person's attitude toward an animal is a critical piece of Laura-Ann's work. She lives in fear of placing dogs in homes where they will be chained outside twenty-four hours a day, which is the way many of them live in Columbia and Greene Counties. People here commonly treat dogs like livestock. Many of these dogs are so loyal that they learn to survive under the grimmest conditions, but this is not the case for all of them. Some slip their collars at every opportunity and arrive at the shelter in terrible condition, eager to shift their allegiances. They become enormously contented once they are treated with kindness and fed on a regular schedule. I come to realize that stray dogs and cats are sometimes not just running, but running away. I no longer view them as lost pets but as refugees looking for new identities and new homes. The shelter offers them a witness-protection program.

Laura-Ann and I go into the back building where the strays are initially kept to take a peek at Nevada. The dog looks old, maybe eight or nine, walks with difficulty, and is covered with some kind of crusty rash. (This turns out to be severe dermatitis, an inflammation of the skin.) He's also much larger than the average retriever. The affable fellow arrived at the shelter dragging a four-foot chain around his neck. The chain, much too tight, had to be cut out of his hair and then clipped off with a wire cutter. "We'll find him a much better home than the one he came from," Laura-Ann assures me. That, I assume, will not be difficult.

Laura-Ann likes dogs but loves cats. She shares her home with five of the furry creatures (and two horses). When the director can't be found in her office, she is more likely to be in one of the cat rooms than cavorting with a dog in a kennel. Nevertheless, Cammisa has recently invited an old terrier named Nicholas to share the front office with Grace and Pebbles. When the dog, a stray, first arrived, he was aged at about six years old. A week later, he was recognized in the kennel by a friend of the family who had originally owned him. Nicholas was really Sparky. When Laura-Ann researched his vet records, she discovered that Nicholas was fourteen years old. He had been in one family his whole life. The old sweet dog was made King of the Pound—shelter mascot. St. Nick lies on the floor in front of the director's office, sleeping most of the day. He loves doughnuts.

Grace, the calico, pops into Cammisa's lap as she hits PLAY on the answering machine to check the morning's calls. As the messages start, Laura-Ann grabs the cat, kissing and hugging her to the point where Grace leaps out of her arms and runs away, her head covered with bright-red lipstick kisses.

Cammisa wants me to learn how to answer the phones and

deal with the public. I have no idea how complicated these generally simple tasks can be in an animal shelter. "Take these down," she tells me as the messages spill out of the machine. I can barely decipher the words, but she is used to the rumble of muffled voices. The first call is from a hysterical woman in Ghent, a nearby town, with an uninvited flock of Canadian geese in her backyard; the geese are terrifying her children and French poodle. She is so upset that she fails to leave a return number. "There's not much you can do about geese, short of getting a Border collie," says Laura-Ann. "There's probably a pond in her backyard. They'll swim, rest, and when they're ready, continue on their way north."

The second call is from Dr. Johnson's office; two cats who were just spayed are ready to be picked up. The third call is from a person reporting a dead dog by the side of the road; a fourth is from a landlord in Catskill, just across the river, complaining about a tenant breeding pit bulls in one of his apartments; the fifth is from a woman in Hudson reporting a vicious, albeit muzzled, German shepherd wandering around her backyard. She sounds frightened and repeats her number twice.

There are more messages, but Laura-Ann suddenly tunes in to a faint sound of crying that seems to be coming from outside. The dogs are making so much noise in their kennels that it's difficult to hear anything through the barking. Laura-Ann turns off the phone machine so we can listen more carefully. The cries are real.

We go outside, and she immediately spots a cardboard box sitting in a flower bed to the right of the shelter door. I expect the worst, even stand back a little, as Laura-Ann rushes over and opens it up. Surprise packages are about as welcome here as a mink coat at a PETA demonstration. (PETA stands for People for the Ethical Treatment of Animals, the largest animal rights organization in the country.)

Inside the box there are nine tiny kittens, maybe one week old, all huddled together on a frayed red towel. Fleas are hopping all over them. The kittens are squealing for food, but there is no mother cat in sight. "Will they survive?" I ask Laura-Ann. "I doubt it," she answers impassively.

The director picks up the box and takes it inside without saying a word. She already has about fifty cats and kittens in residence, which is not unusual in June. The Humane Society of the United States has made June "Adopt-a-Cat Month" because so many kittens are born in the spring. (According to HSUS, the average female cat hits puberty at around 10 months old and can have up to three litters a year. Over a period of seven years, one female cat and her offspring can produce 420,000 cats.) There are four other large litters in the shelter, which is already more kittens than Laura-Ann can put in her main adoption area. "If I fill the cat rooms with kittens, none of our adults will be chosen by adopters," she explains. But the more pressing problem is how this group is going to survive without their mother to nurse them.

The staff is arriving, grabbing the phones as they sit down at their desks. There are three people in the front office, taking calls, accepting surrendered animals, and working on adoptions. A team of four part-time kennel workers cares for the transient population, which ranges from about 50 to 100 animals. At full capacity, the Hudson shelter can hold about 150 animals. While this is the main facility, there is a second smaller shelter across the river in Athens (Greene County), which usually has around 40 dogs and cats for the public to choose from. Space is always kept open for new arrivals in both shelters, which accept animals twenty-four hours a day; no animal is ever turned away. This is the cornerstone of Columbia-Greene's philosophy on animal welfare. Cammisa explains that "people who don't want their animals either neglect them, give them away to inappropriate people, or chain them up in inhumane conditions." She lists these scenarios as if she has repeated them countless times before. "Shelters are the last resort," she adds.

Sometimes Cammisa sounds like an animal rights advocate, but she's not particularly sympathetic to their demands. She supports proactive legislative campaigns but does not engage in local protests against pigeon shoots or the scientific use of animals for research. One of the largest suppliers of laboratory rats and mice in the nation is a breeding facility near the shelter. It's of little concern to the director. She has her hands full taking care of the cats and dogs in the county.

Andrea Walker, the animal-care supervisor, is under twenty-five, has long blond hair, and often dresses in shorts and combat boots; there are no required staff uniforms—yet. Andrea brings the found box of kittens to the examination room. It is her job to examine all the incoming animals and assess their adoptability, which is to say, their health and temperament. After each cat is checked out, he or she is given a distemper shot. Dogs are also vaccinated against parvo, a highly contagious, particularly nasty, and often fatal disease. The dogs and cats are treated for fleas, ear mites, and worms, which plague virtually every incoming animal. Worms are especially hard to get rid of in a shelter environment. There are four common varieties—whip, round, hook, and tape—that can require different treatments. Even though the shelter administers three doses of Panacur, the broadest spectrum an-thelmintic available, the animals frequently pick up another bug during their stay at the shelter and bring it to their adoptive homes. At the moment, Walker is experimenting with a new Bor-detella vaccine, which is supposed to protect the dogs from kennel cough. Upon receiving the dosage, administered through the nose, some of them are coming down with hacking coughs. It takes a few days before their immune systems kick in. Laura-Ann is afraid that the cough will turn off potential adopters, hindering the ani-mals' chances of getting out.

Walker is one of those people born with an extraordinary abil-ity to relate to animals. Not everyone in this line of work has this talent; some eventually acquire it. Walker, however, is a natural. She grew up locally in a close-knit family that included pets. "My parents were permissive," she says. "Our dogs were allowed on the beds." Within the first six months of Andrea's employment, her parents took home two dogs who were in danger of being put down. The first, Marmaduke, was a large, uncontrollable brown dog with some mastiff in the mix, who was going cage-crazy. When Mr. Walker took Marmaduke out for a walk his first night home, the dog pulled him down onto the ground and ran away. Mr. Walker went to the emergency room with a shattered kneecap. (Later that evening, Andrea found the dog.) A week later, Mrs. Walker harnessed herself to Marmaduke, her insurance against losing him, and went for a walk. The dog suddenly took off after a rabbit and Mrs. Walker fell. She was taken away in an ambulance with a bad concussion. The Walkers, undaunted, kept the dog, whom they adore. They even went back for another one. Basil, their second rescue, was a purebred basset hound with a nasty temper. "He's still a monster," adds Andrea. "But they love him."

Walker never imagined herself in a career that would require her to scoop out dog kennels and learn how to inject animals with needles. She wanted to be a stage actress and had even landed a few choice roles in regional productions. But she could not have stumbled onto a more dramatic stage than an animal shelter. She came over one afternoon on a fluke to walk a few dogs—and never left.

This morning's kittens are too young for inoculations. Andrea explains that they won't survive without their mother. She checks to see if there's a nursing cat in the shelter; there are two, but they are busy feeding their own kittens. The other young mothers have been separated from their litters, so their milk is drying up. Still, Walker is determined to figure out some way to save this litter. She asks me to go outside and search the grounds, just in case the mother ran away in fear. "It's their only hope," she tells me.

I spend about twenty minutes looking around. It is a spectacular morning on Humane Society Road; the cows in the field across from the shelter are grazing, and the road is lined with Queen Anne's lace, wild black-eyed Susans, and daisies. There's a red barn in the back and a small paddock where two goats, Billy and Willy, are munching on their breakfast of grain. Billy, the older goat, has swirling horns that jut out of his forehead. Both were seized during cruelty investigations years ago; in exchange for not pressing charges, custody of the animals was given to the shelter—par for the course.

There are several regular outside cats who eat at the shelter's kitchen door. Princess, an eight-year-old black-and-white longhair, is exceptionally beautiful but not too friendly. Fred, an orange male, is completely antisocial. The shelter's outside cats were fixed and released by a previous director; Cammisa doesn't approve of keeping "kitchen cats," as they're called. She feels they set a bad example for the public. The shelter recommends keeping cats inside—all the time—to prolong their lives and keep them from straying. Princess and Fred, however, look perfectly content lying in the sun, licking themselves. Pebbles, who is allowed outside, is another exception to this dictum. A few lonely chickens, strays who became permanent residents, are marching around the animal cemetery, poking at the grass between the headstones. The cemetery is available to the public to bury their animals, but it is so full that there is only room to put ashes in small plots.

The missing mother cat is nowhere to be seen. What if she is hiding in the woods? It's more likely that the person who dropped off this box kept the mother.

When I go back inside to give Walker the bad news, she is crushed. The kittens have been removed from their filthy box, and Andrea is washing the fleas off each of their tiny bodies. She has tried to place them in a cage with one of the lactating mothers, but the cat rejected the orphans. The animal-care supervisor is pressed for time; there are eighteen new animals waiting for their incoming examinations, eight others who need their morning medications, and three cats who need to be transported to the vet for surgery. They've been adopted and are getting spayed or neutered before they go home. There's no time to even begin hand-feeding the kittens. "Laura-Ann doesn't encourage us to keep them alive if there's no mother and they are too small to eat on their own," she says sadly. "Kittens under six weeks old are usually euthanized." It takes me a while to understand the consequences of this piece of reality for kittens in Columbia County.

During the summer, almost three hundred cats arrive each month, a figure that can rise or fall dramatically, depending on whether a collector shows up. "Collectors," in shelter vernacular, are not people who buy art. They are people who take in large numbers of homeless animals regardless of their ability to care for them. Most collectors are eventually turned in to the Humane Society by disgruntled neighbors or landlords when the noise or smell becomes intolerable. Caring for a population of animals is expensive; it's also a full-time job. Collectors usually can't afford to spay and neuter, so their homes become breeding colonies. There are several well-known collectors in Columbia County. When complaints periodically reach a critical mass, a humane officer will get a search warrant and go into their homes to take out the animals. After a bust, collectors frequently move to a new town, where they are unknown, and start collecting all over again. Investigators talk about "depopulating" the same collectors over and over. These cases are extreme, yet they seem to have created a general distrust of all pet owners at the shelter, which I don't quite understand. Again, I have a lot to learn.

"You have to see the most adorable litter that just came in," Walker tells me, lighting up at the very thought of these critters. She wants an excuse to visit with them and takes me into a dilapidated building called "Cat Boarding" that from the outside looks like an abandoned shed. The paint is peeling, the exterior kennels are rusting, and the windows look as if they might fall out of their frames any second. Inside, there's an ancient washer and dryer, several towering piles of frayed blankets, and a large tub used for bathing animals. In another open area, there's a collection of antiquated, jury-rigged cages for about twenty to forty cats, depending on how many can bunk together. Entire litters are kept in the larger cages, while single adults have smaller spaces. The goal is to keep buddies together: the cats are happier, and the shelter can conserve space. There's always a new arrival coming up Humane Society Road.

This is the building where incoming cats initially live. Their first few days are key. The staff interacts with the cats, making notes that will seriously affect whether they live or die. Can they be handled? Do they have any long-term or short-term health problems? Are they making the necessary adjustments to survive shelter life? When a space opens up in the main adoption area, the cats are moved along, one by one, in a system that is geared to getting them out, either through the front door or the back.

The PTS ("put to sleep") rooms occupy an inconspicuous area on one side of the shelter. In one, euthanasia is performed on a table. Then the bodies are taken next door and put in a sealed cold room, where they are stored until they can be cremated. The furnace is in yet another room about ten feet away. This is not a place I visit for months.

Walker leads me directly to a cage filled with a large, stunning longhaired orange-and-white cat. She has almond-shaped green eyes, and she is unusually friendly for a nursing mother. Her four multicolored fur balls are contentedly sucking. "They're all Manxes," she says. "None of them have tails. They came in at about five weeks old, so we've been taking care of them for a few weeks." The litter is so diverse, it's amazing they came from the same uterus; there's a tiger, a buff, an orange-and-white, and a tortie (orange-and-black). "Female cats can get caught by more than one male when they're in heat," Andrea explains. It's difficult to say how many fathers are in this mix. "Laura-Ann has a real weakness for orange cats," she adds, offering me a shelter secret. "Now these babies are eight weeks old and ready to be weaned. They're going into main adoption today. Probably go like hotcakes," she adds, like a proud mother.

We walk back to the office. Andrea reports to Laura-Ann that the "box-kittens" are not doing well and they need to see a vet. "Two cats are waiting to be picked up at Dr. Johnson's office," says the director. "Pick them up, and take the kittens with you." Andrea nods and disappears. I later learn they were too far gone to be saved and the vet euthanized them.

Just as Laura-Ann picks up the phone to make a call, two attractive men in their mid-thirties walk into the shelter. They seem upset. I can tell from their clothes—L. L. Bean and Eddie Bauer—that they are weekenders, probably up from New York. Bill Stone, a redhead, catches my eye and says, "I really feel terrible about this." Laura-Ann looks up from her desk and recognizes him immediately. "Bill, what's the matter with Bandit?" (She remembers the name of virtually every animal she places.)

"Nothing is the matter with him," says Stone. "It's us."

"Are you bringing him back?"

Stone nods solemnly. They've had the dog for only one week. There is nothing more discouraging than an animal being returned, but this dog is coming back for the third time. Bandit looks like an adult, but he's only five months old. A dalmatian-

Akita cross, he's white with a sprinkling of black spots across his thick, short fur. Bandit is the kind of dog that everyone falls in love with because he is so gregarious, but no one wants to bring home. He's huge. At five months, he weighs about eighty pounds. The dog was difficult to place because Akitas have nasty reputations for being animal-aggressive, although people-friendly, while dalmatians, now the flavor-of-the-week thanks to Walt Disney, frequently turn into biters. ("I would rather leave an infant in a room with a pit bull than a dalmatian," a veterinarian once told me.) Bandit's breed combination is not particularly desirable, but he looks like a large version of the RCA dog, which is in his favor. Moreover, his personality is beguiling, the reason he is still alive.

"Phillip is allergic to the dog," Bill tells Laura-Ann. "He had no trouble until we gave Bandit a bath, but a half hour later he had an asthma attack." Bandit, ironically, is happy to be back, wagging his long tail and jumping up on the counter. But Cammisa looks miserable. The more a dog bounces back to the shelter, the harder it is to send him out again. Bill and Phillip are Bandit's fourth owners. Some dogs come back to the shelter and sink into depression; this is not Bandit's problem. The last time he was returned, he kept wagging his tail against the cement walls of his kennel so hard that his tail began to bleed. I soon learn this is a common problem for large exuberant dogs.

As Bill and Phillip leave, a young woman in a nurse's uniform comes rushing through the front door. "I've come to claim my dog," she tells me, frantic. She's late for work at Columbia Memorial Hospital, which is in Hudson, about five minutes from the shelter. "It's a cocker spaniel." I recall an overweight stray cocker sitting in the back kennel. "Is the dog a large blond female?" I ask. "Yes, how long have you had Candy?" I grab the paperwork to try to figure this out.

"How long has she been missing?"

"I just noticed she was gone this morning."

The dog has been at the shelter for four days. One more and she would have been legally available for adoption or euthanasia.

The woman has her act together. She gives me the dog's license, vet records, and enough cash to pay the boarding fees. While she fills out the appropriate forms, I go get Candy, a roly-poly, sweet little creature with a silky coat. When she wags her stubby tail, her entire body vibrates with delight. The dog might be neglected, but she's certainly well fed.

When I bring her out, Candy completely ignores her owner. It's hard to tell if the dog even knows her. But she does know her car and is frantic to jump in and go home.

Purebred cockers—in all colors—come in regularly to Columbia-Greene, usually because they have begun nipping at the youngest child in the household. If cockers were once considered to be one of the most child-friendly breeds, they are so no longer; these dogs have been vastly overbred in puppy mills, which produce the majority of purebred dogs. The term "puppy mill" describes a facility where dogs are bred for quantity, not quality, often in filthy conditions. Pet stores are stocked by these mills, largely because professional breeders would never allow their pups to be sold over-the-counter like shoes. In the animal world, where there is little consensus on most issues, there is general agreement among shelters, breeders, rescuers, and activists that puppy mills should be outlawed. Not only are breed lines ruined, but the dogs are often born with congenital illnesses and poor temperaments. Million-dollar lawsuits over dog bites are not uncommon.

"Until you've been inside a puppy mill," says Laura-Ann, "it's difficult to really comprehend the welfare movement or the shelter mentality about animals. There's a puppy mill currently under surveillance near Troy. I don't know much about it, but if we go in, you can come along—if you can handle it."

"I can handle it," I reassure her, hoping I'm telling the truth.

I begin to wonder if the nippy cockers and cranky terriers whom I meet at Columbia-Greene were produced in factorylike puppy mills. These smaller breeds, regardless of their personalities, get adopted first. But they are far outnumbered by the larger Labrador and shepherd mixes who make up the bulk of the population. This week at Columbia-Greene, there are three adult black Labs and a litter of ten-week-old Lab mixes, a dime a dozen during the summer months. The pups are solid black and look about 90 percent pure. It's impossible to tell what breeds are in the mix when they're so young. There are three males, Picasso, Cezanne, and Mondrian, and one female, O'Keefe. Females are more popular largely because people incorrectly assume they're more docile and sweeter. O'Keefe is adopted her first day out.

All animals in the shelter get named, either when they arrive or at the moment of their incoming exam. The staff will change an animal's name if he or she arrives with one like Devil Dog or Killer. If the animals know their names, the shelter will attempt to find something that sounds similar. If a second Jake or Bear shows up, the newcomer becomes Smiling Bear or Teddy Bear; Jake turns into Jacques or Jacob. You can always count on finding a Bandit or a Lady in the house. One dog who came in named Budweiser became Buddy; a cat named Jerky became Jack; a dog named Stupid became Cupid. I have never met so many black dogs named Blackie or white cats named Casper.

Judging from the population in this shelter, Labradors and shepherds are spreading their seed faster than kudzu. People who breed these dogs don't seem to have noticed the so-called "animal population crisis." But Laura-Ann has. She does not allow dogs, cats, or even rabbits to leave the shelter without being sterilized. Rodents, including hamsters and gerbils, can also be a problem because some vets don't want to operate on them. They're just too small.

When a local vet sterilizes a potbellied pig for the shelter, she tells Laura-Ann that she does not want to do the procedure again because it is too traumatic for the pigs. "Besides," she says, "they live indoors. They're not even kept outside." Laura-Ann explains that the pig she just neutered had been found stray, walking down the road.

Mary Grady bursts through the front door saying, "I know I'm early, but I just couldn't wait." She has an appointment to pick up her new dog, an Italian greyhound named Elmo who is eight months old. The little gray dog has been in the shelter for five days. He was originally surrendered by Jim Cooper, who had purchased Elmo at a mall in nearby Albany. The Coopers just couldn't housebreak him or get him to eat. The dog arrived looking like a Giacometti skeleton.

"Elmo has American Kennel Club papers that came with him at the pet store," Laura-Ann tells Grady. "Would you like to have a copy?"

"What would I use them for, toilet paper?" she responds cynically. Laura-Ann laughs. "People usually want these," she says, waving the certificate around over her head like a flag. "Registering a litter is about as difficult as registering a car," the director informs me, tossing the papers in the garbage. Cammisa thinks the American Kennel Club has promoted casual and rampant breeding; litters, regardless of their size, can be registered for the price of eighteen dollars. (Both parents must also be registered.) She considers breeders to be her worst enemies. She used to have a policy against allowing them to adopt from Columbia-Greene. But over the years she has lightened up. There are many different kinds of breeders, and some of them make outstanding pet owners. In recent years a couple of them have even joined the board of directors.

Andrea walks in with Elmo in her arms. The dog is shaking. Every rib is visible. "I've been feeding him baby food with a spoon," she tells Grady. "He won't eat anything else."

Grady takes one look at this scrawny bundle and sighs with pleasure. She scoops Elmo up in her arms and says, "You have to rock them like babies. I've had a couple of them." A little cloud passes over Laura-Ann's face. "Did you give the others away?" the director casually inquires.

"I've had four husbands," Mary answers right away. "I got rid of each of them, but I'd never give up a dog!" Elmo is already licking her face.

"We have an injured animal in Greenport. Jamie, please get the ambulance ready." The loudspeaker is crackling. "What kind of animal?" asks Jamie, rushing through the office to get directions. "It's a cat that's been hit by a car on Fairway Avenue," Laura-Ann explains quickly. "If it's in really bad shape take it directly to the vet and call me before you make any decisions." Everyone knows what the director means. If the cat is a stray, he or she must be kept alive for five days unless the veterinarian feels the animal will suffer. With any luck, there's an ID tag around the cat's neck. Jamie's out the door.

Jamie Walker, Andrea's younger brother, is a sensitive twenty-one-year-old, with large brown eyes, a ring through one ear, and a full beard that comes and goes. After only a short time at the shelter, he has been proclaimed the most skilled animal handler ever to work there. Like Andrea, he seems to have an instinctive way with dogs and cats, which suggests there just might be a gene for this skill. Jamie is fearless, which is critical to his success with the animals. He is also a philosophy major, on his way to graduate school. This is merely a summer job, or so he thought when he began. Now he's debating whether or not to dedicate his life to animals.

Laura-Ann is surrounded by adopters, and the phones are ringing and ringing. Elise Vega, about thirty and a rock-and-roll singer with a Creole background, is on phone duty. "No, we don't cremate snakes," she says, slamming down the phone. Everybody laughs, and Rocky, her black Chihuahua, who is lying on a small pillow that sits on her desk, jumps up and starts yapping as if he gets the joke, too.

I grab a call. It's the woman who left a message this morning about the German shepherd in her backyard. The shelter is in charge of animal control and collection for Hudson, where this caller resides. Every city or town that licenses dogs is also mandated to pick up and shelter stray or problem ones. Several towns in Columbia County, including Hudson, have hired the Humane Society to do this job. If the woman manages to restrain the shepherd, the shelter is obliged to go get him. (Dog-control officers do not appreciate going out after animals unless they are confined. Chasing loose dogs and cats is rarely successful.) I ask her if she is able to hold the dog, maybe in a garage, until someone can get there. "Are you crazy?" she screams at me. "I'm not getting near that dog, and I don't have a garage. What's wrong with you people!"

I take down her address and tell her that someone will get back to her as soon as possible. She claims to know where the dog lives and gives me the address. Laura-Ann has no one to send right away.

There is a man at the counter who looks familiar. "Elizabeth, what are you doing here?" he asks. Robert Fitzgerald is a writer whom I recently met at an art exhibition in Hudson. I explain that I am volunteering at the shelter and writing about the place. He seems confused, not just about my presence, but about everything. He's obviously going through hard times. Suddenly he begins chatting with me about new art dealers in Soho and undeserving artists who have been catapulted to fame. It's as if we have all day to catch up on the art world. Then he informs me he has a box full of cats in his car. It's ninety-eight degrees outside. "Bring them in right away," I tell him.

Fitzgerald puts a wine box on the counter that is sealed with electrical tape. A few small pencil-sized holes have been poked in the sides. There is no noise coming from the box. "I can't afford to feed them anymore," he says sadly. He finishes filling out the surrender form and then leaves quickly. This is the second surprise package of the day. It might as well be filled with explosives. My daughter, Kate, volunteering with me today, takes one look at the box and runs to find Andrea. They are both horrified when they get the cats out; they're drenched in sweat, panting, covered in their own vomit.

Ten minutes later, Andrea comes back to the office to report that there are six kittens and a young adult, maybe eight months old, who are all dying of hyperthermia. She has soaked them in water to cool them off, but they are only hours away from the end. She wants to rush them up to Dr. Johnson's clinic to see if he can save them.

"Go," says Laura-Ann. "Take them."

While Fitzgerald was chatting with me about the opening of the Whitney Museum's Biennial, the cats were in his car baking.

PEOPLE WHO ARE picking up or surrendering animals come through the shelter at all hours, but the doors open to the general public on the dot of 11:30. Laura-Ann assigns me to the cat rooms, where there are eighteen cages filled with about thirty cats. Some cages contain single adults, others litters, including the prize Manxes. Each cat has a blanket, a litter box, a few toys, food, and water. The cat rooms are bathed in sunlight that streams through the windows. Drawings of animals and lively notes with cat-care tips are pinned to the walls. The attempt to create a happy environment for these unwanted cats almost works.

In the larger cat room, four children, who appear to be related, are pushing their fingers through the cages, loudly dramatizing their affection for the animals. Their mother is rhythmically rocking an infant in her arms while she watches her other kids. She has long brown hair and is wearing tight jeans over a red leotard. The woman looks thin and wasted, twenty-five going on forty. I'm not quite sure why she wants to take care of another living being on top of what looks like an already full house. Her oldest child is about seven, the next one six, five, four, and then the baby in her arms. Cats are not the only ones breeding in Columbia County. The family is noisy, but the cats seem almost to appreciate the fuss; they're meowing, hungry for all the attention they can get. A few of the older cats hang back in their cages, shy of the chaos.

When I introduce myself, Alice tells me she lives in a trailer park about fifteen miles from the shelter in Chatham; her husband, John, is the night janitor at a nursing home. "It's a new job," she tells me without enthusiasm. "He found it through his church group." Alice is twenty-two years old; she gave birth to Craig, her first child, in high school when she was fifteen. The others came soon after, but Alice never married their father. The baby in her arms, her fifth child, is the first she has had with John. Alice is wearing a wedding ring on her finger. "I'm lucky," she says. "John loves all my kids. Before I married him I was living with my parents." Home was an apartment in a development in Hudson, on the edge of the river. "I used to come to this shelter when I was a kid," she says with genuine nostalgia for the place, or maybe for her own childhood. She explains to me that when her father died and her mother remarried, she was forced to move out on her own. Alice was twenty and had four young children. It was around that time that she met John, while participating in a group run by the Jehovah's Witnesses.

While we are talking, the kittens reach out and take random swats at the children's heads with their tiny paws. Alice firmly instructs the children to keep their distance, but they pay her absolutely no attention. When one of them, Paul, gets scratched in the face and begins to cry, his mother falls into a fury, grabs him by the arm, and takes the opportunity to hustle the whole group out the door. "That's it," she says with military authority. She had no intention of adopting a cat. This was simply a family outing to the zoo.

I'm alone in the cat room, so I spend some time with Catskill, my current favorite. He's a big, bushy Maine coon who came in as a stray from Greene County. The cat has a majestic presence; he's the first cat I really want to take home. Then there's Apollo, a large white cat with spots of gray and black on his face. He's sitting on the ledge at the back of his cage, but when anyone approaches, he walks slowly to the front, stretching and yawning. The card at the top of his cage says: "THIS HANDSOME STRAY MIGHT ONCE HAVE BEEN KING OF HIS CASTLE, BUT NOW HE NEEDS A HOME. OLDER CATS ARE WISER, CALMER, AND FREQUENTLY MORE AFFECTIONATE. DON'T PENALIZE APOLLO FOR HIS YEARS." The cat is six years old.

My quality time with Apollo is interrupted by the entrance of two children accompanied by two adults. I am learning to make no assumptions about the kinship ties of shelter visitors. The boy is wearing a Beavis & Butt-head T-shirt, and the little girl has a Barbie cheerleader on her chest. Both kids look under ten. "I want that one," the little girl says, pointing to a calico kitten named Tabitha. The children are moving from cage to cage, as if they are surfing the channels on their television set. Their mother, who doesn't look a day over thirty, is chewing gum and monitoring their distance from the cat cages. She's wearing a flowered pink shift that is skintight on her hefty body; she looks hot and uncomfortable. It's only a matter of time before one of her kids will get scratched. I attempt to warn her. "I know what cats are like," she snaps. It turns out she's not their mother, but their grandmother, baby-sitting on a Saturday afternoon.

The boy suddenly opens up a cage in an attempt to grab Tabitha, allowing Terry, Tommy, Toulouse, and Twyla, her siblings, to run for it. The kittens are elated, the kids laugh hysterically, and the grandmother is enraged. I manage to catch Tommy, but the others scamper all over the room. It's pandemonium time, so I run for help.

Andrea comes into the room and gives me a look of horror that says, "I can't believe you let this happen." She is calm and steady with the kittens, managing to get them all back in their cage in only a few minutes; her tool is a simple piece of string that she drags along the floor for them to chase. Then she turns to the children and begins to lecture them on conduct becoming to a shelter and why they should never open a cage door without permission. Grandma is getting more ticked off; she's the only one who has the right to lecture these kids. Just as she is about to tell Andrea off, Jamie bursts into the room and says there's an incoming litter of eleven puppies (tricolored Labrador-beagle mixes) and he needs her assistance in the examination room. Andrea leaves with him while Beavis and Barbie exit the cat room on their way to check out the dogs in the kennel. I don't want to watch.

Tom LaBuda, one of several part-time cruelty investigators, is in the parking lot, removing two bullmastiff puppies from the shelter ambulance. The pups, about four months old, are goofy and irresistible. Adult mastiffs, usually mixes, come into the shelter now and then, but purebred puppies are unusual. These two, however, have been here before. About a month ago, Romeo and

Juliet came in as strays. The dogs were tied to each other with a rope and were running loose in Greenport, a suburb on the edge of Hudson. When the rope got wrapped around someone's barbecue, creating a racket in their backyard, the Humane Society was called—at three in the morning. Lori and Paul Beckers, well-known animal rescuers who monitor the shelter phones at night, got out of bed to go pick them up. Independent rescuers operate all over the country, saving strays they find themselves or taking in animals from people who must give them up but won't surrender them to shelters where they might be euthanized.

Lori Beckers is the patron saint of older animals in Columbia County. She began rescuing frogs and other insects as a child, moving on to a parade of dogs, cats, horses, pigs, and cows, among other creatures. At the age of forty, most of her adult life has been spent working with animals. Her husband, Paul, also loves animals, which is why he is still her husband. Lori cannot pass by a shelter without visiting the animals and making a donation on their behalf. On a recent trip to Massachusetts, she pulled over to check out a local facility; there was a rat on death row. Now Ben sits in a big cage in her living room.

"You wouldn't believe where these mastiffs came from," LaBuda tells me. He's in a sweat, and he's really pissed off. Tom loves animals, but airplanes and guns are his real passion. He supports his family by working as a night guard in a housing project in Troy. LaBuda was on his way home after working all night when he received a radio call from the Hudson police who had responded to a complaint about two abandoned dogs. When LaBuda went to investigate, he found the mastiffs tied up behind a two-story house. The front door to an apartment on the first floor was wide open, displaying two rooms covered in feces and completely trashed by the dogs.

The neighbor who called the police claimed that the dogs had been alone with no food or water for three days. The police officer who entered the apartment was so appalled by the mess that he called Tom to come right over and take the dogs to the shelter. Their owner, Bobbie Ann Slade, was nowhere to be found.

Tom is going back to take pictures of the scene so I go along. Wendy Reed, the neighbor who phoned the police, is standing outside a small gray house, about a hundred feet from a Pizza Hut. She looks worried. "Bobbie Ann's been gone for three days," she tells us. "It's not like her to leave the dogs alone." Wendy has long, stringy hair and is covered with paint. She's helping her husband paint a hairdresser shop in town because she just got laid off from her own job at a drugstore in a nearby shopping center. When I peer into the window of Bobbie Ann's house, the mess is truly awesome. The dogs have pulled everything possible out of cabinets, drawers, and shelves. Every piece of furniture has been shredded, and there is garbage strewn over the floor. These pups must have had a really good time.

"I didn't have enough money to buy any dog food for them," Wendy explains. "But when I gave them water, they nearly leaped into the bowl." She is the one who removed them from the wreckage and chained them in the back of the building where their owner regularly tied them up. When LaBuda got to the dogs, maybe eight hours later, the chain was wrapped around the male's neck so tight he was gasping for air; eventually he would have strangled himself. The female could not get up because one leg was caught in the chain. But now they're both fine. Back at the shelter they dine greedily on huge bowls of food.

Bob Grazianno, the dog-control officer for a significant chunk of Columbia County, is bringing in a stray Siberian husky, with one blue eye and one brown one, found running on the Taconic State Parkway. The dog is in bad shape. He's thin, limping, and his coat is filthy, but he's extremely affectionate. Huskies, bred in abundance by numerous local breeders, frequently turn up at the shelter; even breeders bring them in when the dogs aren't sold or are returned to them. Elise Vega takes one look at this husky and names him Grover. It's a perfect fit. I assume that given his obvious charm, Grover will be adopted quickly, despite his limp. In the beginning, I assume that virtually all the dogs will be adopted quickly.

Barbara Spataro, the investigator on duty, is finally returning this morning's call about the so-called "vicious" shepherd. Spataro is a small, attractive woman, with a short, functional haircut. She has taken part of the requisite training to become a peace officer. Peace officers, as humane agents are called, are required to participate in forty hours of classroom work and forty-eight hours of firearms training. Spataro has done the classroom work, but she is not licensed to use a weapon because she has no desire to carry one. Spataro, therefore, cannot make arrests, but she can give out warning slips and send the police in to make arrests.

Lee DeLisle, the chief investigator who runs the cruelty division, is an ex–police officer from Albany. He gladly carries a gun and might have difficulty deciding which one out of his collection to pack in the morning. DeLisle grew up north of Albany in Cohoes, where he says the term "gun control" refers to "the ability to hit your target." Cohoes is famous for being the place where Hiawatha, the fictitious Iroquois chief of schoolbook literary fame, died. The legend goes that he went over a waterfall in a bark canoe, screaming "*Cohoes!*" as he fell to his death. As a child, Lee was told that *Cohoes* translates into "help," but he grew up thinking it really meant, "Oh, shit."

Much of DeLisle's time at the shelter is spent checking a range of complaints that are phoned in by the public. Currently on his desk there are reports on illegal cockfights, a herd of dead fallow deer (raised domestically for venison), a pit bull breeder selling dogs for sport in Hudson, abused elephants at the Catskill Game Farm, and hack horses with no shelter at the Ponderosa Fun Park in Greene County.

Spataro gets many of the garden-variety dog and cat cases to follow up. Not only does she know the particular shepherd accused of terrorizing the neighborhood this morning, but she knows precisely where he lives; she's been there before. Spataro agrees to take me along, and we drive off in the shelter ambulance, which is filled with cages, blankets, a pole (a nylon lasso attached to the end of a metal rod, used to catch aggressive or sick animals), and a radio hooked up to the shelter.

Hudson is a city of eight thousand people, built on a hill that runs right down to the river. On a clear day, the Catskill Mountains are visible from the town square. The city, which is the county seat, has a reputation for superb eighteenth- and nineteenth-century architecture. Hudson was originally settled by Quakers in 1783. By the turn of the century, prior to the discovery of petroleum, Hudson was organized around an active wharf and a lucrative whale oil business. Eventually the railroad cut off the harbor from the rest of the town, and the river reverted to the status of landscape. The residents turned to manufacturing; Hudson became known for its ironworks, quality carriage makers, and overflowing breweries. Warren Street, the main drag, is well cobbled and lined with antique stores and quaint replicas of old streetlamps. But poverty is just a block or two away in any direction. Employment is scarce, and Hudson, like New York City, is plagued with drugs and pit bulls.

Columbia Street, where Spataro and I are going, was once Diamond Street, named after Legs Diamond, a renowned bootlegger who supplied the area with booze during Prohibition. At one time the street was lined with brothels. Today the same buildings remain, but they're more dilapidated.

The Packards live in a small wooden house that might have been built a hundred years ago. It's literally falling apart. Spataro was called to their home about a year ago on a previous complaint about a limping black dog that had allegedly been beaten by Mr. Packard. When Spataro got there, there was an old black dog tied in the yard, but he appeared to be in decent health. "Decent" is the operative word. Animals cannot be taken away from their owners on first inspection unless the animal is near death, a condition that must be verified by a veterinarian, or the shelter can be sued for stealing or trespassing. Veterinarians, however, are not anxious to get involved; they dislike being placed in the middle of domestic disputes or arguments about the "quality of life" for a pet that are difficult to win.

When Spataro and I arrive, the Packards' three boys, roughly ages two to five, are playing outside near a large purebred German shepherd; there's no black dog. The shepherd is on a six-foot chain attached to a fence. His only shelter is a run-down doghouse that looks as if it was hastily knocked together out of wood scraps. There's a filthy blue blanket tumbling out of it. Near this structure are two metal bowls; one is empty, and the other is turned over.

The oldest of the children has cuts all over his legs that are dirty, bleeding, and unbandaged, but Spataro is there to consider the health of the dog, not the boys. Shane is an unneutered male, maybe nine months old. He's quite active on the chain, moving around and around the perimeter of the space available to him. Mrs. Packard looks about twenty-five years old. She has a tan, weathered face. Her thin body is barely covered by a bright blue tank top and denim cutoffs, and her teeth are stained. They protrude slightly from her mouth. When she begins to speak, her voice has a distinctly southern twang.

Mrs. Packard greets Spataro politely, and the investigator quietly explains why she is here and describes the complaint that has come in to the shelter about the shepherd. The woman seems surprised. She claims the dog is never taken off his chain, not even to come in at night; he sleeps outside all year. She suggests that her neighbor is confusing her dog with another shepherd down the street who barks incessantly and frequently gets loose. Just at that moment, as if on cue, a dog barks down the street. Mrs. Packard grins at this miraculous Hollywood moment. Her story is absolutely plausible.

As Mrs. Packard continues to speak, her youngest son, who has spiky white-blond hair, tugs at his mother's shirt to get her attention. "Shane knows how to escape!" he says, and disappears himself. Mrs. Packard is a little embarrassed but still cool. She confesses that she has no idea what happens when she is at work. A muzzle for the dog is hanging on a hook by the door. As she explains the reason for the muzzle, the same child walks over to the dog and simply lets him off the chain, as if this were routine. Mrs. Packard appears shocked but doesn't reprimand the child. It's as if she is a visitor in her own backyard. The boy laughs, then throws a ball for the grateful dog. The front and back gates to the yard are wide open.

The dog is energetic but much too thin. When let loose, he doesn't seem to know quite where to go. It takes almost a minute before he bounds over to me, insistently sniffing my legs as if I were a choice fillet. Spataro notices that his ears are covered with bloody scabs, which look to be infested with small bugs, gnats or flies. I am appalled, but the investigator is blasé; she's seen it all before. She explains to Mrs. Packard, who claims to be rubbing Vaseline into the animal's ears, that this is a common problem for outside dogs. Once flies begin to bite in a certain area, the spot can begin to attract more insects. Spataro suggests an inexpensive treatment, a balm, readily available in stores.

Just then, the children bring a white kitten from the house. They want to display all their animals, as if this were show-and-tell time. The whole family is enamored of this blue-eyed, longhaired, white kitten—Kitty, they call her. But Mrs. Packard is starting to lose her patience with the children and our intrusion. "That's my baby," she says sternly, pointing to the kitten. "He's not allowed outside of the house, and the dog is not allowed in."

Spataro quickly brings the conversation back to the dogs. Where's the black dog? "We put him to sleep," explains Mrs. Packard. "He was old, and Shane is more relaxed without him around." The investigator asks if the dog frequently knocks over his water bowl. Yes. She suggests nailing the bowl to the side of his doghouse. Then she hands Mrs. Packard a warning slip. The woman is not impressed; she takes it as casually as if she were receiving a receipt at the grocery store, turns around, and goes into her house. We leave right away.

This is a difficult case. It presents Spataro, and hence the shelter, with an insoluble dilemma. The shepherd is not in bad enough shape for Spataro to consider seizing him. Yet she knows that outside dogs on chains do not fare well. It's only a matter of time before they escape and get into trouble—bite someone, run in front of a car, get sick. Yet, in the country, this is the way many people keep their dogs. Spataro spends much of her time dealing with the ones who get tied up and twisted on short leads to the point where they are in danger of strangulation, starvation, or dehydration. Nevertheless, there is no law against leaving a dog tied outside twenty-four hours a day if the dog has some shelter (legally, a tree is sufficient) and is fed and watered. But inevitably these are the dogs who end up at shelters. They become the unwanted. Once an animal's health begins to fail or the people move to a place with no yard, the dog gets left behind—or needlessly put to sleep, like the Packards' black dog, who was traded in for a new model. Shane is at the beginning of this cycle.

Perhaps the black dog is better off dead than alive living life on the end of a short chain with little food. Or is life—even under the harshest conditions—better for an animal than death? This dog, for me, is at the heart of the dilemma for every shelter employee. There is more than enough evidence to guess that Shane, like his predecessor, will not do well in this family. Yet people certainly have the right to raise their pets without interference from a social agency.

The Humane Society of the United States, the national organization located in Washington, D.C., that offers guidelines for local shelters, argues that euthanasia is by far the more humane choice when the quality of life for an animal does not meet basic standards. But defining "quality of life" is a little like defining the word "obscene." One person's obscenity is another's passion, art, even. People in Hudson, as elsewhere, keep their dogs on chains outside. To them, just the idea that the "quality" of a dog's life can be grounds for seizing their animal seems like an absurdity. As a result, many people in Columbia County think the animal shelter is run by fanatics.

The Packards' shepherd is still young and energetic. He's an expensive, beautiful dog purchased from a breeder; his ears are perfectly pointed and upright, and his eyes radiate intelligence. Spataro and I discuss the dog's chances for adoption at the shelter. I presume, as usual, that he would not be difficult to place; she's not sure. But either way, the investigator doesn't have the right to take him at this point. "He's not sick enough," she says.

"What about the bugs on his ears?"

"They're hardly life-threatening. If your dog had an infection in his ears, would you appreciate the Humane Society coming onto your property and taking him away?" The investigator has a point. Driving back to the shelter, I realize there is not much to be done for Shane. "Much of what we do is prevention of further cruelty," explains Spataro. The Humane Society sets a standard for the quality of life through its adoption policies, but enforcing the standards in the community is difficult. "At least the Packards know I'm watching," she says, "That's all I can do."

In the two hours that Spataro and I were gone, fourteen animals have been surrendered to the shelter. There are ten new cats and four new dogs, including a three-month-old harlequin Dane and two boxers. Camille Praga, a kennel supervisor, has the boxers outside in the parking lot. They look so robust and healthy that at first I assume they must be visiting the place. Camille sets me straight. Buster and Samantha, brother and sister, are two-year-olds who have never been separated. Their owner has a terminal illness and can't manage them anymore.

Toby, the Great Dane, was purchased for a child's sixth birthday from a local breeder. Darcy Lewis paid $1,500 for the black-and-white spotted puppy. But whenever Toby lay down on the floor, the three-year-old in the family attempted to mount the dog as if he were a horse. The dog began nipping at the kids to keep them away. The woman was scared; the kids turned against the dog. She was advised to get him out of her house before the nips turned into bites. When the breeder refused to return her money, she brought Toby to the shelter. The dog has been in residence for just two hours and there are already three applications on him. Toby is a prize.

IT'S ALMOST FIVE, and the staff is getting ready to call it a day. The sign on the front door now reads CLOSED, but there is someone knocking furiously. "I've got animals!" shouts the woman at the door. She's on crutches. When I open the door, I realize that she is crying. It's hard to tell if she's overwhelmed with emotion or with pain.

Janet Cole has been living on her own for two years, since the age of eighteen. She has bangs and a blond ponytail; her face is red and blotchy. A month ago, she was in a devastating car accident. Janet ended up in the hospital for three weeks; she lost her job at Wal-Mart and then her apartment. Now she has been forced to move back to her parents' home. They are happy to take in their daughter, but not her cats. Janet has two tigers, Betty and Veronica, who are her closest companions. She weeps at the thought of losing the only things she has left—her cats. Janet wants to know if the shelter can keep them until she recovers and finds work, maybe a month or two.

This is a tough question, especially during the summer, when animals are pouring into the shelter like water from an open faucet. The place is operating at full capacity, which is difficult for the small staff and an obvious financial burden. The shelter can't board animals—there's just no room. If Janet leaves them off, anything can happen; the cats may be adopted, separately or together. Or they may get sick, not necessarily with a terminal illness, but with any one of numerous infections that cats pass around. There is an upper respiratory virus currently going through the cat areas that has been a chronic problem for months. This disease is so contagious that visitors and employees are asked to wash their hands in between handling each cat. Cammisa can't give Janet any guarantees. She can't even be encouraging. The only way to make sure that an animal will survive at Columbia-Greene Humane Society is to take that animal home.

Out the window, I can see Betty and Veronica sitting in the car with Janet's father. His hat is pulled down over his eyes, and his mouth is set in a slight frown. Janet is still crying, trying to compose herself. Laura-Ann turns to me and says, "Go on out and talk to him, maybe you can convince him that it's too dangerous to leave the cats here." I look at her like she's nuts. "Please try and talk to him," Janet pleads. For the moment, she's stopped crying. How can I refuse?

I walk outside slowly. I'm not that great with my own father, but you never know. "You must be Mr. Cole," I say to the man. He shoves his hat back a little off his face and nods. The cats, stuffed into a small carrier, are crying. I can't read the man's face, but his body language is telling me to go away. "What a terrible accident," I comment. "Poor Janet." He nods again, still mute. The man is like a rock, but he must have a crack somewhere. I open the back door of his car, as if I'm going to remove the carrier, but instead I peer in and take a closer look at the cats. "They sure look like nice cats," I tell him. He is looking at me, waiting for me to take these creatures out of his life. But instead of obliging him, I slam the door closed and move closer to the driver's window where he's sitting.

"Look," I tell him cautiously, "your daughter has just lost her apartment, her job, and very nearly her life. She needs her cats to help her heal. If you leave them here, they may be dead or gone by the time she wants them back." I pause. Mr. Cole is staring at me, confounded by my comments. "This is your chance to be a hero. Janet is crying inside the office. Let her take these cats home." The rock isn't moving. We're holding each other's eyes in silence, but I can sense the debate going on in his head. Do I have the right to tell him what to do? Then, finally, the rock begins to crumble. He takes his hat off, rubs his fingers through his hair, and says, "OK. Tell her she can keep her cats." I thank him profusely and walk back to the office with good news. A minute later, Janet comes running out of the shelter, her crutches flying, to give her father the hug of his life. We are all watching through the window, vicariously sharing her joy. Betty and Veronica are going home.

Benjamin, one of
Laura-Ann Cammisa's five cats

TWO

Cat People

It's NINE O'CLOCK in the morning and a large sign on the front door makes it clear that the shelter does not open to the public for another two and a half hours. Nevertheless, two nuns are anxiously banging on the door, shouting, "Hello! Hello!!" Who could refuse nuns? I open the door, and they explain that they are in dire need of an ambitious mouser. "The church has filled with mice," one of the Sisters tells me in a melodic Irish brogue. "We had a stray for five years who did an excellent job, but he passed away last week, and we're already overrun."

With Laura-Ann's blessings, I take them right into the cat rooms, which have already been cleaned. At this hour, the nuns have the place to themselves. The Sisters methodically peer into every cage: the first cat is too old; the second one is too big; another is too thin. I'm not sure why I assumed that nuns looking for a mouser might be fairly easy to please. These women are carefully considering each cat, reading the narratives on the cards out loud to each other. Then they come across the Beatles—Ringo, Paul, John, and George—four picture-perfect tigers with stripes on their backs and spots on their bellies. One of the nuns confesses that she always liked George the best and asks me to take out the cat named after him. "I liked George, too," I tell her. "But I switched over to John."

As I open the cage door about an inch wide, all four kittens scramble onto the floor in a blur of fur. I manage to grab George by the scruff of his neck, but the others run under the cages, leaping around the floor as if they were in gymnastics class. I'm hoping the nuns are amused. I'm an obvious neophyte, but they don't seem to mind. I hand George to one of them while John begins climbing up the other woman's leg, digging his nails into her stocking. "Ouch!" she shrieks. "They're too feisty. Put them back!"

It takes a few minutes, but with the help of some cat toys, I round up the rest of the band and return them to their cage. Thanks to Andrea, I have learned how to outsmart eight-week-old kittens.

The nuns move on to Apollo, who is looking calm and regal in comparison to the Fab Four. But it's hard to know if Apollo would do well in a church or whether he even considers mice to be a challenge. Yet he's the kind of cat who has the build of a potential hunter; he looks strong and sly. I push Apollo, god of sunlight. The nuns are interested. When I open up the cage, instead of running out, he slowly strides forward, stretching as if taking a bow, and then he sits down at the edge of the cage, waiting for someone to lift him up. This is one classy cat. I carry him over to a table in the room so both women can stroke him.

I can tell they like the cat right away. He's rubbing up against their arms, soaking up their attention like a plant starved for water. I decide to leave them alone. Apollo doesn't need me to point out his finer points.

The truth is, when I first began volunteering at the shelter, I viewed myself as a dog person rather than a cat person, and I assumed most people fell into one category or the other. I had friends who were obsessed with their cats, while I bonded mostly with dog people, discussing training, groomers, safe toys, and city dog walkers. While I had lived with a few cats over the course of my life, I had never really scrutinized the species or studied their language.

Laura-Ann took it upon herself to teach me about cats. Once I knew, for instance, that cats have over forty muscles in each ear, I had a new appreciation for their sensitivity to sound. Cats also have scent glands around their mouths, foreheads, and near the base of their tails, where they like to be rubbed. I began to reflect on the dexterity of their movements and the nuances of their language. And when I started to distinguish meows from purrs and contented felines from depressed ones, I had more access to the complexity of cat culture. Laura-Ann invited me to meet her own cats, who live in a place known around the shelter as the "Cat Palace." Staffers joke that they want to be born again as one of Laura-Ann's pampered cats. Her house is really their house.

Laura-Ann is a quintessential cat person, but at the shelter she manages to keep her passion relatively in check. In the privacy of her own home, however, her affection for cats knows no bounds. The director surrounds herself with cat art, cat dishes, cat quilts, and cat things, creating an intensely feline atmosphere. Every inch of wall space is covered by an image of a smiling cat, with a few cows and horses thrown in for good measure, and there are stand-up figurines perched in corners or creeping along available railings. Even the bathrooms are filled with prints of happy-go-lucky creatures, mostly cats.

As soon as Laura-Ann walks through her front door, she begins a dialogue with her four cats, who are usually scattered all over, out of sight. At the sound of her voice, they come out slowly, one by one. The cats are too spoiled to simply throw themselves at their mistress. They hang back, waiting to be coaxed out. Laura-Ann speaks to them in a sweet, singsong voice, the kind a parent might use with a particularly bewitching toddler. After about five minutes or so, the cats finally deign to present themselves, looking to be fed. They gather in the kitchen, leaping all over the counters and the stove.

Can cats be trained to stay off the counters? They can. But Laura-Ann says, "If you don't want a cat on your kitchen counter, you probably shouldn't have a cat at all." Her own cats have been known to sit with her at the dining-room table and eat off her plate.

Laura-Ann's cats are a motley group, all blossoming in her care. Cary (named after Grant) is a nonchalant, sturdy gray-and-white male; Benjamin is a wiry orange-and-white cat who easily dominates the others; Brandon is an orange-and-white giant who gets along with every living thing; and Lily, a shy calico, is Laura-Ann's baby.

Figuring out why this woman is so attached to cats is not simple. "My mother loved cats," she tells me, "but they were never the center of the household." She has two significant memories from her childhood when the seeds of her obsession began to grow. Laura-Ann remembers refusing to watch Westerns on television with her father because she was so afraid the horses might trip. When her uncle filled his freezer with rabbits he had shot one season, he invited the relatives into the kitchen to show off his catch. Laura-Ann closed her eyes.

As a child, however, Cammisa was dreaming not about animals but nuns. "That's what all good little Catholic girls dream about," she tells me, as if I should already know this fact. Born in Brooklyn, in 1949, she was the first of three daughters in a close-knit Italian family. Her father was studying to be a civil engineer, while her mother took care of the kids in their basement apartment on Lancaster Avenue. "It was all we could afford," she remembers. But life improved when the family moved to Massapequa Park, Long Island, largely to take advantage of the public school system.

Cammisa went on to Catholic college, where she learned more about independence than faith, and immediately flew off to Italy for a year as soon as school was out. By 1972, she was twenty-three years old, weighed one hundred pounds, and was five feet two inches tall. Her waist-length hair bounced freely down her back in a look that was unequivocally feminine, giving her a decided edge for certain kinds of employment. Despite the budding women's movement, the airlines were aggressively hiring the svelte and shapely to fly the friendly skies. Laura-Ann took the bait.

"I knew I could physically meet the criteria to become a stewardess, so I applied for a job at a couple of airlines," she remembers. "The interviews were unbelievable. At Pan American, we had to parade up and down a hallway so the executives could check out our legs." They liked her legs, but Laura-Ann went with Eastern, flying off to its training camp in Miami. "I thought it would be a dream come true," she admits. "I had just returned from Italy, and all I wanted was to get back to Europe. I longed to travel, if you can believe that," she says with a laugh. It is difficult. The woman I know is phobic about planes and hates leaving home for a single night. I can't even get her to go out to the movies.

Stewardess school was a total bust. "It was like joining the army, except we were being trained in femininity," she continues. "When we arrived we were each given a makeup kit from Christian Dior, so we were all wearing the same pink lipstick and pink nail polish. Then they began instructing us in how to shave our armpits and use vaginal sprays. It was the seventies! Women were talking about liberation, and Eastern was teaching us how to please businessmen." Alice in Wonderland was waking up to smell the coffee, and it was being served by Stepford wives.

Laura-Ann's moment of truth arrived when it was her turn for a makeover. The powers that be insisted that she cut off her magical tresses. "I had brought a wig with me because I knew my hair would be an issue," she explains. But her mentors weren't interested in making an exception. "I hadn't cut my hair since I was sixteen years old, and I wasn't going to do it to please Eastern Airlines," Laura-Ann says. She quit the program and flew home to New York.

By 1977, Laura-Ann was living on the Upper West Side of New York City in a studio apartment with over a hundred potted plants. "It took her hours just to water them," says Jeff Schloss, the man she later married in 1980. Schloss was an actor making his living as a waiter. "When I first got to know Laura-Ann, she had a small catering business. She could cook a meal for two hundred people in a kitchen that was so tiny you could stand in the middle and touch all four walls."

Cammisa was renowned in the neighborhood not for her love of cats but for her ability to bake pies, cobblers, tarts, and mousses, which she sold to local bakeries and restaurants. She remembers a bake-off sponsored by Abraham and Strauss, where she entered her pumpkin cheesecake, a tasty, puddinglike confection, the color of mud. "Jeff and I were standing in a subway station on our way to A&S and I dropped the cheesecake on the platform! We couldn't piece it back together so I ran to a deli, bought some sour cream, and covered the top with it." The pie won second place. Had it not been slathered with a layer of sour cream, the cheese-cake probably would have come in first, as it did a year later in a contest sponsored by a local block association. Laura-Ann won a clock radio.

Her extreme passion for animals, especially cats, developed later, with a stray she found in Manhattan outside her apartment building. Behind her landlord's back (although with his wife's blessings), she took Linus in and fell deeply in love. Yes, with a cat. When she talks about this big orange creature, it's as if she were speaking about her own child. There was something about her re-lationship with Linus, their ability to comfort each other, that moved her in a way she had simply never been moved before. Per-haps Linus was a notably intelligent cat; maybe he was just ex-traordinarily grateful. Either way, Linus marked a turning point in

Laura-Ann's life, leading her to become part of a loosely organized group of women who rescued, fostered, and found homes for city strays. She took in cats and a few dogs, including a cherished husky mix named Hobo. When she couldn't place any of these animals in foster care or move them into permanent homes, she took them to a shelter run by the ASPCA (American Society for the Prevention of Cruelty to Animals). "I was grateful that I had a place to bring them, and I never questioned what happened to them," she says, looking back on her own naïveté. Now she knows what happens to strays who end up in shelters, especially in New York City.

When Cammisa speaks about her life prior to working with animals, it's as if she is talking about a distant relative, now deceased. At times she talks about the days when she would spend all evening cooking, seeing friends, or doing calligraphy, one of her secret skills. But gradually her obsession with animals slowly took over her life, filling up each and every hour of her day. "Do you believe I used to be a creative person?" she asks mournfully. Now all her creative energy is poured into her home (she still has innumerable potted plants) and her cats.

Light streams into this contemporary, cedar-and-glass house from numerous windows, bathing the cats, who sun themselves on cushions and in baskets, which are strategically placed for their pleasure; Laura-Ann put in a special bay window with a platform seat to enable the group to closely watch the birds. They are not allowed outside—ever. But the cats don't seem to mind their confinement. Why should they? There are colorful pillows, blankets, and toys tossed all over the place to make a thoughtfully constructed cat playground. This privileged group of cats has paid its dues; each has been pulled back from the brink of death at the shelter. Now they inhabit a cat utopia where creature comforts have priority over human ones.

"I was visiting Laura-Ann once and I was about to sit down in a comfortable chair in the middle of her living room," says Lee DeLisle, relishing this story. "But Lily was sitting there. So I started to pick her up and move her off the chair, as any normal person might, and Laura-Ann had a fit. 'No one is allowed to disrupt a cat in this house.'" DeLisle kids the director, one of his closest friends, about her animal obsessions. He is a frequent visitor to her house because one of Laura-Ann's horses, Dakota, belongs to him; Honey, Dakota's companion, was a gift from him to her. Horses must always have at least one animal companion (a goat will suffice) because they do not do well alone. Dakota and Honey move together, eat together, and sleep together; they are also bathed, shod, and vetted together.

Lee comes over to ride Dakota now and then, but Honey is somewhat green; she's never been thoroughly "started" (the politically correct term for broken). When Laura-Ann sent her out (along with Dakota, of course) to a trainer for a few months, she took them back before the work was finished after the horses came down with coughs. Laura-Ann has little interest in learning how to ride although she has taken a few lessons—she offers photographs as evidence. But the shelter director remains ambivalent about continuing Honey's training. Her horses are purely pets, not working animals. "I'm not convinced that horses are happier working," she says. "People assume this is the case, but no one really knows. Horses are certainly not unhappy playing and eating all day long." Who can argue with that?

DeLisle can. "Breaking a horse is critical," he says. "It can affect

their future. It's dangerous to have a horse who can't be handled."
But Lee has learned not to get into (too many) philosophical arguments about animals with Laura-Ann. Despite their work together, and their friendship, they have different views on the
subject. Their disagreements, however, do not prevent him from
leaving his beloved horse in her care. The paddock where Dakota
and Honey live is spotless; when Laura-Ann is around, she shovels
manure several times a day. The horses sleep on fresh cedar shavings, cleaned every evening, and are fed a special mixture of grain
and vitamin supplements. For snacks they get homemade cookies,
filled with carrot shavings and molasses.

At the end of the day, Laura-Ann looks forward to coming
home and shoveling manure in her peaceable kingdom. She has
not added a new animal to this group in three years. Her last addition was a longhaired stray who showed up for supper at her back
door. The director took the cat to a veterinarian and treated her to
the works—shots, a leukemia test, and a spay. The cat was given
the distinguished name of Tootsie and brought to the shelter office
for a few days. But Grace, the mascot calico, was not pleased with
the addition, although Pebbles, Grace's buddy, didn't care one way
or the other. Nevertheless, Laura-Ann brought Tootsie back home,
where she became the director's one and only inside-outside cat.

Tootsie ventures into the mudroom at Laura-Ann's house, but
that's as far inside as she gets. The cat is pampered like the inside
four but never invited in to join them. Laura-Ann is convinced
that Tootsie would upset the balance of personalities. When cats
have territorial fights, they often begin urinating outside their
boxes. One shelter board member with several cats ran a twenty-
four-hour video camera in her kitchen to find out which one of

her crew was peeing illicitly. Every cat in Laura-Ann's home has a separate litter box, which is one secret to maintaining harmony in a group; there are also four separate bowls (crystal, naturally) of water on Laura-Ann's kitchen floor.

After spending some time at the Cat Palace, it was clear to me what was missing in my own life. At this tender moment in my developing cat-consciousness, I began to feel badly for a tiny white kitten named Tibbs, with a ferocious upper respiratory infection, who was sitting in isolation at the shelter. Tibbs had already been adopted by a family, but right after his neuter surgery, he became sick, probably because he had been incubating an infection. (This is why shelter animals frequently come down with something the minute they get to their new homes; their immune systems crash during spay or neuter surgery, so budding illnesses immediately blossom.) Tibbs's adoptive family was waiting for him to recover, but the little guy just kept on coughing and crying. He needed to get out of the shelter and recover in a catless foster home. I was told his condition would clear up in two weeks, so I took him home.

Three months later, when the cat finally stopped gagging, he was no longer a cute little kitten. His adopters wanted a baby; they chose another shelter kitten. I certainly had no desire to give up my cat.

Tibbs had already begun to teach me the advantages of cats over dogs. Cats, for instance, are content being cats, while most dogs I know, including Snowy, are wanna-be people. Cats know how to keep human beings in perspective. It's not that they don't appreciate us, but that they prefer to live without too much interference. Cats seem to have enough going on in their own lives to keep them relatively uninterested in ours. This is hardly the case with dogs.

Tibbs finds much of what Snowy does to be very peculiar. For instance, the cat would never consider eating an entire box of raw pasta—box included. Nor would he try to chew on a lightbulb. The difference between cats and dogs is a little like the difference between baseball and football. They're both equally popular, but in the latter, the head is primarily used as a battering ram. Dogs are children. Cats are artists.

The average cat owner, with an affectionate tabby or two, probably does not realize that there are dozens of distinct cat breeds, as well as cat shows that occur with just as much fanfare as the canine variety. These events give breeders a chance to show off their prize pupils and, of course, take orders for kittens, which can be sold for hundreds, even thousands, of dollars.

My arrival at the Columbia-Greene Humane Society was the beginning of my education. I assumed, like most people, that purebred cats did not end up at shelters. They're too expensive, too valuable, too precious—right? Then I started to meet the Siamese, Himalayan, Persian, Balinese, and Maine coon cats; the Manxes, Japanese bobtails, Ocicats, Russian blues, and Turkish Angoras who were occasional guests. They were strays, just like the tigers and other shorthairs.

One morning in the shelter, I pick up the phone and it is a woman who wants to report a cruelty. This is Barbara Dohrman's bailiwick, but she is frantically trying to pay bills, order dog food, find someone to fix the washing machine—again—and the accountant is already on hold waiting for her. Dohrman, who originally moved to the area from New Jersey, has worked at the shelter for more than five years, running the office. She nods eagerly when I offer to take the call for her. I have not yet learned that the simple act of answering the phone, especially on a cruelty, frequently implies the acceptance of some responsibility for an animal in trouble in Columbia or Greene County.

"I don't know if I should be calling the Humane Society," a voice whispers.

"Why not?" I respond.

"Because I'm a breeder, and I know you folks don't like breeders." We chat a little, and I find out that she breeds Himalayan and Persian cats. This woman has no idea how lucky she is that I took her call; Laura-Ann eats cat breeders for breakfast, and Dohrman doesn't have time to listen to their problems. The caller is nervous and will not give me her name or phone number, which I need before I take the report. I tell her that our conversation will be moot unless she is willing to identify herself, and she gets miffed. I back up, promise her anonymity, and explain that the cruelty investigator might need to get in touch with her again. She's still unsure. When I suggest that we terminate the conversation until she makes up her mind, she decides to spill her story.

The caller describes a woman who had been cat shopping for a Persian in the area who finally showed up at her place. The shopper described one particular breeder who had over forty cats in a trailer; she claimed the cats were stuffed into filthy cages and all very sick. "The only reason I'm calling the Humane Society is that I love Persians and I think they deserve better," the caller tells me.

"Why didn't the woman call in a complaint herself?" I ask.

"She didn't really care enough about the cats to get involved," the woman says.

"How do you know the cats are really sick?" I ask. "You haven't seen them with your own eyes."

"I spoke with her at length," she insists. "I know she was telling the truth. Why would I risk my reputation as a breeder by calling you if I didn't think there was a real problem?"

I put her on hold for a minute and consult with Dohrman, who says right away that I need to talk directly to the woman who saw the cats; this is all hearsay.

"I need to speak with the person who saw the cats," I tell her, back on the phone.

"I'm really sorry," she says apologetically. "But I promised her I wouldn't give out her name." She agrees to encourage the woman to call the shelter, but she's doubtful about the results. Then she gives me the precise location of the trailer and the breeder's name. "This is all I can do," she says.

Laura-Ann is so skeptical about this complaint that she barely wants to hear about it. The director is not particularly fond of Persians, or any purebreds. "This is just one breeder ratting on another," she says dismissively. "Wouldn't this woman be thrilled if the Humane Society went in and closed down a competitor?"

But I'm not convinced. "I have no one to send out there, anyway," Laura-Ann says in an attempt to conclude the conversation. "Why don't you go," she suddenly suggests. "Wouldn't Tibbs like a Persian companion?" Maybe he would.

There are two Persians sitting in the cat room right now. One of them is a mix who came in as a stray with his foot caught in a leghold trap; he was promptly named Trapper. These are steel traps, hidden in the woods by hunters, that look like large sets of false (but sharp) teeth. When an animal steps on one, the trap snaps shut, usually breaking every bone in its way. Leghold traps are illegal in some states because they are considered inhumane. Moreover, they often catch domestic pets rather than wild animals. Trapper got off easy. His leg wasn't hurt, and he only had one toe amputated.

I tell my daughter, who spends a lot of time with me at the shelter, about the cruelty report from the cat breeder, and she immediately cooks up a plan. "You call her up and tell her that you want to buy a cat for your daughter. It's her birthday, and you want to bring her over to pick one out." Kate wants to do some detective work. "I'll point to the sickest ones in the cages so we can take them out and check their eyes," she adds. "Then I'll look in their ears." Kate knows what's she's doing around cats after having spent some time in the shelter's examination room, and I would definitely rather have her with me than go in alone. But I am not fond of situations where I knowingly misrepresent myself and encourage my daughter to do the same. I explain the ethical dilemma to Kate, who has a solution to every problem. "Then buy me one of the cats for my birthday," she suggests hopefully. Her birthday really is coming up, and this is the back end of her scenario.

When I reach Denise Abbott on the phone, she tells me she has about twenty Persian and Himalayan kittens available for sale. Abbott encourages me to set up an appointment quickly because she's having a summer sale. "My place is a mess," she warns me. "I'm remodeling my trailer." She goes on to explain that she was recently divorced and is working full-time in sales at a toy store. "That's how I pay for my cats," she adds. I can sense the constrictions on her life in the economy of her words. The woman needs to sell off some cats to sneak by.

Laura-Ann suggests that I make an appointment to see the cats and then show up at the right time, but a day early. That way, Abbott won't have a chance to clean up the place, move the sickest cats out of sight. But somehow I can't bring myself to do this. I'm already setting her up.

Kate and I have a difficult time finding the right trailer park in Valatie (birthplace of Snowy), and then the right trailer once we are in the park. When we finally do, we are half an hour late; Abbott is upset because she has left work to accommodate us. She's wearing a yellow polyester suit, lots of makeup, and has short, tightly curled blond hair.

We enter her trailer. It's not a cat palace, but it's not a cat dungeon, either. It is, indeed, a mess; half of it is under construction and being painted. In a little alcove, there are about twelve cages filled to the brim with cats; some cages have four adults in them, which gives them no room to move around. "I leave the air-conditioning on for the cats," she tells us. "They hate the heat." These cats have long hair and pushed-in faces. Persians are prone to eye problems, and many of Abbott's have goo under their eyes and red streaks down their faces. "You have to wash their faces every day," the breeder explains. Then why don't you? I want to say.

Abbott has not cleaned up the place for us or even scooped her litter boxes. But, beyond the clutter, her cats look lethargic, matted, and unkempt. Healthy, active cats keep themselves groomed. "When I sell one, I clean her up and groom her," she explains. "I don't have time to keep them all brushed." Then Abbott interviews us about how we keep our pets. If we want one of hers, we will be asked to have the cat spayed or neutered. "My cats should never be allowed outside," she adds.

Kate is wandering around, picking up loose kittens off the floor, and poking fingers into cages, just like other children she has watched at the shelter. Abbott is watching her out of the corner of her eye. "I want to see that one," Kate says to me, pointing out a large gray kitten who looks somewhat abject, sitting in a corner of a cage. Abbott takes him out for us. "He's thin," I comment. "He's just active," she tells us. "That one's a real live wire." Kate is giving me a look which says, "Let's take him." I can't tell if she's acting or not.

"Do you have any other cats?" I ask, fishing for a hint of another stash. "No," she says, "This is it." She explains her price structure: "Three hundred dollars for a cat with papers and $150 for one without. If you want to show or breed, you'll need the papers, but otherwise they're not much good." When I tell her I need to think over the decision, she hustles us out the door, quickly locks up the place, and is out the driveway before Kate and I have our seat belts buckled. There's an outbuilding behind her trailer, and I'm tempted to go peek in the window, but I am concerned that neighbors might be watching. I notice that Abbott has left the air-conditioning on for the cats, all forty-six of them.

When I describe the scene to Laura-Ann, she thinks it's borderline, not bad enough to go back in with a search warrant. "At least she asked you to fix the cat and keep it inside," she adds. I sadly agree. Denise Abbott is a small-time breeder who is not adequately controlling her population. She's stuck with too many cats, too many kittens, too many bills, and not enough time to even keep the cats clean and looking decent. Breeding is not always a lucrative business. Over the next few months, the shelter gets in several Persians, and I begin to recognize Abbott's line. So does the kennel staff; they all have drippy eyes.

I CANNOT COMPREHEND why Catskill, a magnificent Maine coon, has been sitting in the shelter for months. When my friend Sandra Kingsbury, a teacher in New York, comes in with her daughter, Nell, to choose a cat, I'm hoping they'll go for him. Catskill is a subtle cat dressed in a fancy costume. His personality is laid back, but his presence is huge. Sandra and Nell spend hours trying to choose a cat, which is always the sign of a serious pet person. First they want Sasha, then Squid, then maybe Catskill. But in the end, Nell wants an adorable longhaired kitten named Ashley. Who can blame her? Catskill is a little shy, and Ashley needs a home, too.

Cats outnumber dogs by three to one in shelters across the country. Unlike dogs, they are generally not licensed, but in recent years, county health officials have mandated that they receive rabies vaccinations. (Several small towns are currently experimenting with licensing requirements for cats.) People, much to my amazement, assume that cats can do just fine living on their own. In the country, feeding a stray at the back door is routine. A few of these cats might get taken in, but most of them just keep breeding under porches and in the woods. The result is a pack of feral cats in the yard.

Wild cats are a significant problem in New York State, in both rural and more densely populated areas. Catching them requires skill, not to mention courage. These cats are impossible to touch, let alone put in a carrier and take to a veterinarian's office. (Most vets don't look forward to handling them, either.) Feral cats frequently hang around dairy farms, but given the falling price of milk, farmers aren't inclined to put much care into them. When cats become a bother, people call the Humane Society, a nuisance-control service, or they get out their rifles and shoot them.

Feral cats are not enamored of people, either. The shelter offers the community humane Havahart traps, which must be set with food and water and regularly monitored. Getting the cats into the traps is easier than taking them out. This is a skilled job that some shelter workers won't even go near; new staffers have been known to hide when batches of feral cats arrive. The cats have to be transferred to cages where they can be fed and watched for a few days, but in the process, they have a tendency to fly out of the traps and go for the nearest face.

Andrea Walker and Camille Praga, the part-time kennel supervisor, can get them into cages without a scratch; they place the end of the closed trap in an open cage, so the cat has nowhere else to go. But sometimes these cats escape, like Houdini, and must be caught with tongs. Lori has scars on her arms from going after them with her hands.

"Some feral cats make good barn cats," says Dr. Susan M. Tanner, a local veterinarian in Old Chatham who tries to work with cat rescue groups. "But only if they are spayed or neutered and vaccinated," she says. "These cats proliferate like crazy." Cammisa doesn't participate in any programs to save feral cats or release them into controlled colonies; they are all euthanized after their five days of stray time. As a result of this policy, there are certain cat people who will not set foot in the shelter. Many of them believe that no animals should be euthanized. From Laura-Ann's point of view, putting a feral cat up for adoption would be insane. "Not only do they hate being caged, but who would want to adopt a feral cat when there are forty friendly ones available?" explains the director.

The shoppers I see cruising through the shelter do not want wild animals. In fact, quite the opposite. They are looking for best friends—beautiful, healthy, well-behaved perfect pets. That's what I wanted when I initially walked into the shelter. But they don't exist. Great pets are made, not born.

Shelter workers and rescuers understand the cat problem, but the general public seems completely oblivious. Once I see the dozens of cats coming into the shelter, week after week, I can't understand how people can merrily surrender their cats and kittens—purebreds, calicos, oranges, blacks, whites—without acknowledging an iota of responsibility for bringing them into the world. The average person wants their precious cat to have at least one litter; the assumption is that giving birth is good for the animal. Moreover, the children want kittens, and the parents think that the process will be a valuable lesson in the joys of reproduction. This fantasy, however, is fueled by myths. Unneutered cats are more vulnerable to testicular cancer. They will also spray urine all over the house. For females, a spay surgery can prevent breast cancer; sterilization also helps keep unwanted male admirers at a distance. Giving birth is not a risk-free process for people or for animals. Thousands of kittens, born in happy households, end up in shelters because their owners can't give them away. How can shelters be expected to place them all?

When the same people bring in litter after litter, they do not expect to be reprimanded or lectured. Still, as I listen to Cammisa insisting that a surrenderer sit still for a crash course in pet over-population, I realize that she is not just a knee-jerk animal ideo-logue. If she can persuade one person to spay or neuter a cat, it will lessen the load on her own staff down the line.

Every once in a while I watch Laura-Ann convince a person not to surrender the cat that is waiting right outside in the car. She seems to have developed powers of X-ray vision that enable her to see into people's hearts and minds to sort out truths from half-truths and outright lies. Laura-Ann can separate the decent pet owners from the borderline ones in only a few minutes of conver-sation; she also watches how they physically handle their own dogs and cats at the shelter. She teaches me how to selectively head off incoming animals over the phone. When someone calls to ask about bringing in a cat who is urinating outside the litter box, I ask, "Do you always use the same brand of litter?" If they say, "Yes," which is the usual answer, I advise them to change brands and keep the cat for a week. Eventually, we segue into a discussion of urinary tract infections and allergies. The goal is to get the caller to take the cat to a vet—not a shelter. People do not realize that vet-erinarians can be instrumental in solving a multitude of behav-ioral problems that begin as medical ones.

There's a message on my home machine from Sandra Kings-bury. I immediately assume the worst, which is the shelter state of mind when an adopter calls out of the blue. But Sandra reports that Ashley is fine—a sweet, affectionate critter who has moved in with no trouble. The problem is, she can't get Catskill out of her mind. I am familiar with this problem myself. "If he's still sitting in that small cage," she says, "I just can't stand it."

"He's still there, waiting for you," I tell her eagerly. There could be no better home. And by the end of the week, Catskill has moved in with Ashley.

ONE NIGHT, after everyone has left the shelter, I watch Laura-Ann sneak into the cat room. She really does try to treat each cat in the facility as if he or she were her own. She talks to them in her funny voice, makes sure each one has a toy and a blanket before she leaves, opens up each cage, and gives every cat a kiss good night on his or her cheek. Inevitably, she covers them with her signature lipstick marks, which the morning staff will chuckle over.

Cage by cage, this is a time-consuming ritual that appears to relieve some of her own anxiety at the end of the day. The cats know her; Oliver, who doesn't give me the time of day, runs up to Laura-Ann, and she counts the six toes on each of his front feet as if this were a regular routine. The director makes a point of checking Gemini's spay scar; George's ears; and all their nails, which are supposed to be kept short. "Cats with long, sharp nails get adopted last," she says. I realize she's not only checking the animals, but checking up on her staff. She points out misspelled words on two cage cards and complains about some dirt in the corner of the room. "I'm not even going to open up the supply closet," she adds. "I'd just get upset."

When we get to Apollo's cage, there's a large Siamese mix named King Tut sitting in it instead. My stomach tightens. "Where is he?" I ask nervously. "Relax," she says. "He's not in heaven, but close to it." The nuns picked him up a few days ago.

Buster and Samantha

THREE

You *Can* Go Home Again

ANTHONY LAWRENCE, thirtysomething, is standing at the counter filling out a surrender sheet on his dog. Lawrence is heavy, beginning to lose his hair, and wearing a T-shirt with a picture of a giant frog in the process of swallowing a beer can. New animals are greeted with a mixture of curiosity and apprehension. I walk outside to see a stately springer spaniel, liver-and-white, sitting patiently in a rundown Honda Civic. The dog wags his tail eagerly as I pass by and catch his eye. When Lawrence comes out, he tells me the dog is a stray whom he found in Hudson two weeks ago. His landlord insisted that he get rid of the dog; the Lawrences already have a large Labrador. He seems quite attached to this springer, whom his son named Pip. He tells the shelter that the dog is six years old. "He has a few warts and a skin problem, but it's no big deal," he adds. Lawrence requests some time alone with Pip before giving him up. "Pip slept in bed with my son," he says. "We got attached to him pretty quickly."

I leave the man and his dog to bid each other farewell in private and go back into the office, where there are new people I do not recognize. The turnover is so fast that fresh faces appear weekly. Andrea Walker is still here, but she's leaving soon. She's decided to go for a Veterinarian Technician license, which requires two years of school. Vet techs, well trained and less expensive to employ than doctors, are frequently the workhorses in veterinarian practices and shelters. The techs can do almost everything but surgery. Laura-Ann spends almost 50 percent of her time hiring new staff and figuring out how to get rid of problematic current employees.

I grab a phone to help out in the front office and am stumped on the first call. It's an older woman with an incontinent twelve-year-old Pomeranian; the dog is in diapers, and she's fed up caring for her. She wants to know if we will put "Rosie" up for adoption, or just "kill her right away." I put the woman on hold and get Laura-Ann.

"What should I tell her?" I ask.

"Ask her if she's going to get rid of her husband when he becomes old and incontinent," the director growls. Then she picks up the phone herself and tells the woman that putting her old sick dog in a shelter for her last few months of life would be an act of cruelty. "Old dogs, especially those with health problems, should not have to make this transition," she explains. "First of all, this is a noisy and frightening place for elderly animals. Second of all, few people can afford to adopt a dog that's sick. The medical bills are prohibitive. The kindest thing you can do, if you love your dog, is have your own vet put her quietly to sleep in your own home. Save her the trauma of coming here." The caller begins to cry. Laura-Ann sighs loudly. "If you can't do it," she continues, "we will have to." There's the answer to her original question. But this is one dog I have the good fortune never to meet.

Lawrence is still outside having trouble separating from Pip. He wants to take the dog into the back kennel himself to see where Pip will be kept. This is not an unusual request, but the building is for staff only. Some of the dogs inside have not yet been examined or are aggressive. At the moment, Grover is there, along with Toby, a litter of eight Lab-rottie pups, three stray Lab-shepherd mixes, a German shepherd named Prince, a Siberian husky named Lady Luck, a small gray terrier named Smokey, and the two mastiff pups held as evidence on a cruelty case, who are growing up in the shelter. There are only three empty spaces left, and one is going to Pip. I am wondering where they are going to put the animals if there's a sudden rush.

In my first few months of volunteering in adoption services, I want to quickly give dogs and cats to everyone who walks in the place, before space runs out. My feeling is that Cammisa and her staff spend too long agonizing over the placements and have difficulty letting go of the animals. There is endless debate about whether one family or another is good enough to get Smokey or Grover. They are so used to the reality of euthanasia that they are no longer frightened by it, whereas I see it as a constant threat. I start calling up my friends to come in and adopt animals, but my friends think I've gone over the edge. I disparage the staff because

I conclude that many of them are more inclined to distrust strange humans than strange animals. Cammisa feels I don't quite understand either the community or her policies. "But you will eventually," she tells me. "We all go through the same stages. I used to feel exactly the way you feel now."

I decide to track some dogs from the first moment they enter the system, to see what determines whether they are adopted or not. There is not much method to my investigation; I pick dogs whom I happen to observe going through the initial trauma of entering the shelter. For me, surprisingly, this turns out to be a bonding experience. The payoff is the tremendous pleasure I feel when the dogs get placed. But the pleasure is too often short-lived. A significant number of dogs come right back again and have to be placed for a second or third time. Whenever the returns start mounting, Cammisa wants to tighten adoption procedures. But holding dogs in a shelter when a possible home is waiting makes no sense.

Anthony Lawrence and Pip get my attention right away because even though this man is attached to his dog, he is letting him go. I wonder if Mr. Lawrence has tried to find a home for the springer before bringing him in. I go outside for the third time to get the dog and see that Lawrence is crying. "Pip will be set up in the main adoption kennel as soon as there is a space," I say, trying to comfort him. "Purebred dogs tend to get adopted first." He reluctantly hands me the leash, embarrassed by his flood of emotion.

"I have an idea," I suggest spontaneously. He looks up at me. "Would you like the shelter to call your landlord and try to work it out? Maybe we can help change his mind?"

"No," he says adamantly, as if my offer to help is offensive. "Don't do that." Then he abruptly gets in his car and drives away, never looking back.

Pip is a real sport, nowhere near as upset as his owner about their parting—at least not yet. I bring the dog into the office to find a member of the kennel staff to take him in. "Where'd you get *him*?" Lori Beckers asks rhetorically, giving the dog a pat on his head. "Nice warts," she adds. I tell her about the long farewell with Pip's weeping owner, and she says, "Yeah, yeah, yeah. If he was really that upset why didn't he keep the darn dog and get rid of the landlord?"

Lori is wearing a T-shirt that reads "I'VE CALLED IN SICK SO MANY TIMES, THIS MORNING I CALLED IN DEAD." At forty years old, she is far and away the shelter employee with the most tenure—sixteen years—and the best sense of humor. Lori can be totally wicked, which is why most people prefer to stay on her good side. She usually says precisely what's on her mind and will go to any length to save an animal. When there's an emergency, she and her husband, Paul, are always the first to arrive on the scene. Her latest adventure involved rescuing a bunch of cats from a burning tenement. The fire marshal called in the middle of the night, and the Beckers were rousted from their bed to save the injured and dispose of the dead. Over the years Lori has pulled horses out of rivers, cows out of swamps, rats out of euthanasia rooms, and dogs and cats out of just about everywhere.

Once, when Lori was on a routine cruelty investigation involving a dog chained to a tree, she found an old, malnourished Labrador who had no shelter or water. But the really bad news was that some male dog had nailed her while she was tethered; she had a dozen newborns to feed. This really ticked Lori off, and there was no way she was going to leave this starving mother tied to the tree with her babies. When the investigator informed the family that she was taking their dogs, the youngest boy, maybe six years old, started swearing at her and kicking up a fuss. Lori pulled a gun on him and shut him up. She then calmly proceeded to load all thirteen dogs into the shelter ambulance. The incident earned her the sobriquet "Becker the Wrecker."

Lori left an indelible impression on the boy, now about eight. "That fuckin' lady came with a gun," he told me three years later. I had returned to the same house with investigator DeLisle when the shelter received more complaints about the family's current dog. This time around, their dog was fine. A neighbor had called in the complaint, hoping the Humane Society would harass them. "It's the Montagues and Capulets," DeLisle said to me as we left the scene. The family was relieved to see DeLisle rather than Beckers, who eventually was phased out of cruelty work more for health reasons—Lori suffers from severe asthma and allergies—than her bulldozer style.

When I remind Lori about this particular incident, she doesn't quite remember the family but has a vague recollection of a white dog and puppies. "If I took the dogs with me, you better believe I had a good reason," she says. I believe her.

Lori loves animals more than she loves most people, a fact she enjoys broadcasting to just about anyone. "You won't believe this," she says to me. "We just got in a five-year-old black Lab, a really nice dog," she adds. "Look what her owner wrote." Lori hands me the incoming form so I can read it for myself. In a delicate script, under "reason for surrender," the dog's owner wrote, "No room in the backyard."

"I asked her how big her yard was," Lori continues. "She says, 'Well, it's pretty big, but we just put in a swimming pool so there's no more room for the dog.' That's a new one, isn't it?" Lori laughs, shaking her head. "It's a real nice dog, too," she repeats. Lori is known for her appreciation of older dogs. I am told that her house is like a canine geriatric ward.

"Are you interested in adopting the dog?" I ask her.

"Maybe," she says. "But I have five at home already, and you should see my kitchen at feeding time." Then she describes a dinner ritual that is so tightly choreographed it sounds like a Merce Cunningham piece. "Come over sometime," she says as she answers a phone.

Andrea takes Pip into the back so he can get some breakfast. The dogs are howling (there are four beagles in residence) and scarfing down their food as if there is no tomorrow. Meals, of course, are the main event in a shelter dog's life. The sound of twenty dogs eating voraciously, licking their metal bowls clean, and slurping down water to cleanse their palates pleases the kennel staff because it's an indication of the animals' good health and high spirits. When the dogs don't eat, the staff has to figure out why. Shelter dogs are generally appreciative of any attention they receive.

After the dogs finish breakfast, they anxiously wait for Fred Bernockie, a retired mailman from Hudson, who gives each one of them a twenty-minute walk up Humane Society Road, past the cornfields and cow pastures. Fred is a volunteer; he walks every dog in the facility seven days a week, without fail, in all kinds of weather, as if he were still delivering the mail. When this ageless gentleman comes through the kennel with his frayed yellow lasso (a makeshift leash that gives the dogs about a six-foot lead), each dog goes nuts, animated by the hope that Fred is coming for him or her next. It's not as if they don't get other walks during the day from potential adopters or staff members, but the dogs worship Fred. One adopter brought a little West Highland terrier back for a visit with Fred because she thought the dog needed cheering up. On occasion there's a rare dog in the shelter who is so aggressive that even Fred can't get near him or her. More often there's a hastily handwritten note on a kennel that says: "DANGER—ONLY FRED CAN HANDLE." Fred has no fear of animals. He is also virtually deaf—no liability in his line of work.

Fred comes into the front office to find out which dogs are going home today, because he will give them baths. "Going home" is a phrase that chimes through the shelter like wedding bells. When the dogs actually leave, it's a big event; staffers come out to say good-bye and give them kisses and hugs. Zack is about to be picked up, so Fred will give him the first bath. Zack is a genial two-year-old tricolored wirehaired terrier mix who is straight out of *Annie*. He's going home with the Salts and their six children, who range in age from four months to fourteen years. Priscilla Salt, who looks to be in her late twenties, has her hands full, but not just with the kids. Jim Salt is over six feet and is as difficult as he is tall. On his first visit to the shelter, he irritated every staff member who dealt with him. As far as Jim was concerned, filling out an application to adopt a dog was a ridiculous procedure.

When the Salts' car pulls into the parking lot, there's a collective groan in the office. "Guess we can't like all the adopters," says Sue Spohler, preparing herself for the coming ordeal. Spohler is one of the most valuable and flexible staff members. She is calm and firm, generally able to handle a range of personality types. Unlike Beckers, Spohler has some affection reserved for people. She has a warm, upbeat personality and a head full of fabulous strawberry blond hair. Spohler lives ten miles up the road with Cody, her eight-year-old son, and five—at last count—Manx cats. In her spare time Sue makes colorful jewelry, much of which contains whimsical animal and vegetable imagery. (I, myself, own a curvacious beet that makes an occasional appearance on my lapel.)

Zack has been at the shelter for twenty-two days waiting for someone to take him home. Personally, I really go for the shaggy terriers, and I'm surprised when they sit in the kennel for weeks. These are the first people who have looked at Zack twice. "Let's hope it works," says Laura-Ann. "It wasn't a bad application."

The Salts walk through the door briskly. They're in a rush. They're annoyed that they had to bother driving over to a nearby town clerk's office to get a license for the dog. Andrea brings out Zack, who is looking clean and fluffy. She begins to talk to them about the dog's care; everyone gets a little speech on the basics before they walk out the door. I'm watching Jim from inside the office as he repeatedly interrupts Andrea, making it difficult for her to finish a sentence. Andrea's getting annoyed. She gives up on the lecture, hands Priscilla the leash, and walks away.

"I can't deal with him," Andrea says to me in the privacy of the office. "All I'm trying to explain to them is how to take care of the dog's neuter scar, and the man won't shut up. How did these people get through adoptions?" she asks. "They think they know everything about dogs because they bought a dachshund at a pet store that they gave away in less than two months! Zack is too good for them." These are not nice people. But they have the right to own a dog, and they made it through the shelter's hurdles.

I walk out to greet the Salts and bid farewell to Zack. In the process, I remind Priscilla that Zack is a little bossy. "He *is* a terrier," I explain. "You better give him a chance to adjust, especially to all your kids." She nods at me, and while we're chatting she warns her kids not to maul the dog. "Don't let them near him while he's eating," I caution her. Any dog, not just a terrier, can be overly protective of its food around children and other animals.

Priscilla wants some information on dog food before they leave. I ask her where they shop because I want to figure out a brand of food that will be convenient for a mother of six to buy.

"Why do you want to know where we shop?" Jim interrupts, as if I've asked his wife to reveal a coveted family secret.

"There are average dog foods distributed through supermarkets," I explain a little defensively, "and quality brands distributed through stores like Agway and True Value, where you might already shop."

"I don't give my kids *quality* food, so why should I feed it to the dog?" Mr. Salt replies.

I can't tell if I'm supposed to be amused or not. Priscilla looks at me sheepishly and says, "He's just joking."

"What do you feed the kids?" I ask him, begging for another punch line.

"Macaroni and cheese," he says. "Every night. Let's get out of here." He signals Priscilla to move, and she hustles the group out the door with Zack's leash in one hand and the baby in her arms.

A year ago my sympathies would have resided exclusively with Priscilla; now I feel for the dog, too, because I know he'll be at the bottom of the Salt totem pole.

Everyone is worried about Zack. Laura-Ann is looking over the application again. "They got through because there were no concrete reasons to deny these people a dog," she tells the staff. "They were even honest about giving away their last puppy," she adds.

"Do you have the right to deny people a dog simply because you don't like them?" I ask.

"We're a private agency. We can do whatever we want," says the director. "But I like to have a real reason when I deny someone a dog. It's not that we don't automatically deny many people. Look at the Warning List. It's thirteen volumes long." The Warning List is an alphabetized directory of people who will never have the privilege of adopting an animal from the shelter. Most of them have surrendered abused animals or had animals taken from them.

The Columbia-Greene Humane Society's adoption requirements are stricter than some shelters and more lax than others. The local shelter in Ulster County, across the river and south of Greene County, does not place animals in homes outside the county. I would have been denied a dog there because 212's are not welcome. At another shelter, just outside of Albany, adopters can drop in, choose a cat or dog, and walk out with their new pet in twenty minutes; nor are the animals spayed or neutered before they go home.

One afternoon, while observing the flow of animals and people at New York City's Center for Animal Care and Control, I watched a Russian couple with no English, and living on a subsidized income, adopt a little unneutered dog. The couple had been in this country for less than six months and had never previously owned a pet. When the adoption counselor handed them a certificate, giving them a free neuter surgery at one of numerous veterinarians' offices that service the shelter, the adopters looked absolutely blank. In an effort to explain the meaning of the surgical procedure, the counselor picked up the small dog and pointed to his genitals, repeating the word "neuter" several times and making a cutting movement with his hand. But this gesture seemed to get the adopters even more upset. They were firmly shaking their heads saying, "Nyet. Nyet. Nyet."

Then I began to wonder if these people might think they were being asked to castrate the dog. When I suggested this to the counselor, a lightbulb went off and he rushed outside to get the couple's son, a man of about thirty-five, who spoke some English. The son appeared to understand the confusion and was enlisted to explain the distinction between sterilization and castration. He spoke to his parents in Russian, and after a while his father calmed down. He reluctantly accepted the certificate as if it were a subpoena to appear in court.

After the family left with the dog, leashed on a collar and chain that, minutes earlier, had been taken off another's neck, I asked the counselor why he thought these people would give this dog a good home. He answered, "When they walked through the kennel, they looked at the dog with great love in their eyes."

"That's your main criterion?"

He nodded.

"Will you follow up on the dog?"

"We don't have time," the exhausted counselor explained. Then he told me sadly that the little dog would have been put down that evening. The constant pressure to place the animals before they are euthanized makes it difficult to keep them from slipping through the cracks.

Two days after going home Zack is returned to the shelter. Priscilla walks in carrying her two-year-old, who has a small cut over her eye. "It wasn't Zack's fault," her mother insists right away. The little girl had come up from behind the dog, who turned quickly and accidentally nicked her in the face. The child had been hysterical. "We just can't keep him," she says with genuine remorse. The Salts want their money back, which they are entitled to because they have returned the dog within two weeks. The little girl wants to look at other dogs, but Priscilla has the good sense to tell her, "No way."

When one of the adoption counselors, a British woman named Andrea Stewart, announces that she is considering taking Zack home, it seems to start a landslide. Suddenly, after he languished in the shelter for weeks, Zack is everybody's choice; there are two new applications on the dog by the end of the week. I realize that there really is no accounting for taste, no scientific formula to figure out what dogs are going to be adopted by which people. Some weeks, I surmise that all the small young light-colored dogs get adopted first, but then a little white puppy is left at the shelter for three months before going home. Some weeks, everyone is looking for a nonshedding terrier or poodle mix, but then Rocky, a purebred standard poodle with a heart of gold, is in the kennel for almost four months. When he finally goes home (with the owners of one of the largest cattle farms in the area), Elise Vega weeps, she is so happy for the dog. She had been taking him home at night for periodic sleepovers at her apartment to cheer him up.

Both applications for Zack offer him great homes, so the shelter has the luxury of choosing one of them. Zack is sent to live with a family where he fits in right away with the parents, two children, and his new best friend, a feisty cocker spaniel.

WALKER IS WORRIED about Pip, the six-year-old springer who has been around for several weeks. The dog is getting visibly depressed, lying down in his kennel all day, his nose between his paws. Dogs are pack animals, but being locked up in a noisy kennel is especially stressful for older animals. Puppies do best in shelters; they play all day with their littermates until they drop from exhaustion. Older dogs, however, have had enough experience in various homes to know what they are missing. Pip is becoming lethargic and losing some fur, along with his interest in people. No one walking through the place looks at him because he lies low in the back of his cage; a springer rescue group (every breed has a group of dedicated fans who rush to the rescue of individual dogs) has not even had the courtesy to return the shelter's calls for assistance. When dogs are around for a while, the staff will begin to strategize ways to protect them from euthanasia. I watch Andrea spend her lunch hours with Pip, walking and talking to him, sharing her food with him.

"Why don't you just bring him home?" I finally ask her.

"Oh," she says. "I guess I haven't told you about Peanut." Peanut is her difficult golden retriever mix who doesn't get along with other dogs, or warm up to people, either, for that matter. He bit a close friend of Andrea's in the face. ("It wasn't the dog's fault," she says.) Peanut was rescued from an abusive family that was giving him away for free at their yard sale. Andrea is devoted, but Peanut is so neurotic that she can't bring Pip, or any other dog, home to join them.

The shelter is chock-full, and euthanasia decisions will soon have to be made. Andrea goes to Laura-Ann and begs her to move Pip into the office for a week. Since Nicholas, the beloved office mascot, has quietly passed away, a spot in the front office is open for a dog. "If it works out, we might want to keep him there," Andrea suggests, fully realizing that mascot animals are protected from danger.

Laura-Ann is God with the power of life or death over these animals. This time around, God grants Andrea her wish. Much to his delight, Pip is moved out of the main dog kennel and into the office, where a bed is put down for him on the floor. Laura-Ann still has Nicholas's ashes on her desk; she hasn't had time to order him a headstone.

The third day Pip is in the office, Mr. Volk, an elderly German man who barely speaks English, calls up because he and his wife have just lost their twelve-year-old springer spaniel. They are grieving and looking for another dog. "It's a miracle," says Barbara Dohrman, who has taken a shine to the old spaniel who has been living under her desk. When the Volks hear about Pip they, too, consider the match to be a miracle. They rush over to the shelter to meet him.

The Volks are in their eighties. They speak and move in slow motion and are looking for a calm, quiet dog. Mr. Volk is able to speak some English, but his wife, a demure woman under five feet, speaks only German. They were caretakers on a large estate in Old

Chatham for almost forty years. Now they've retired to a log cabin in Ghent. They want to take Pip home immediately. They think he even looks like their old dog, Fritz.

Elise is processing their application, and she has some concerns about the placement. "The Volks' last dog was tied up outside for most of the day," she tells Laura-Ann. "But they brought him inside at night," she adds hopefully. After speaking with their references, Elise becomes more sympathetic to the elderly couple. "They're both home during the day, and Pip will be with them. Mrs. Volk fed her last dog the same food she cooked for themselves," she adds.

"What did she cook?" I ask.

"Hot dogs, mostly," says Elise, sticking out her tongue and making a face. She's a vegetarian. The Volks are not the kind of people who are interested in the nutritional distinctions between Iams and Gravy Train, but their dog was treated like a family member. "Let's give them the dog," says Laura-Ann. "He deserves a real home." Even Andrea is thrilled. She personally drives him to the vet to be neutered.

Dr. Johnson calls Laura-Ann immediately following Pip's operation. The vets rarely call unless there is a problem. "He came through like a champ, but this dog isn't six years old," he tells the director. "He's probably ten or eleven." Laura-Ann is stunned, along with the rest of us. Pip is pretty energetic for such an old dog. But surgery at that age requires special consideration. Dr. Johnson isn't pleased with the error. "But if he was concerned, why didn't he call me before the surgery?" wonders Laura-Ann.

As it turns out, Pip is healthy and returns from the hospital in good spirits. But the Volks need to be told the dog's real age. "There is something strange going on here," says Elise. "This discrepancy is suspicious." She wants to poke around a little, get more information on the dog. Although Pip came in as a stray, the finder seemed positive about his age. Elise decides to give Lawrence a call.

Lawrence's mother answers the phone. "We just want to tell you that we found Pip a good home," says Elise cheerfully. Mrs. Lawrence is thrilled. "Do you remember what year you got the dog? There's been some confusion about his age." Mrs. Lawrence pauses and replies, "Well, let's see. We got Pip the same year my grandson was born, so that makes him about eleven years old." Elise, who has been working in the animal welfare movement most of her adult life, is livid. She informs Mrs. Lawrence that her son lied to the shelter about the dog's age and turned Pip in as a six-year-old stray. "He jeopardized the dog's life in surgery, and now his potential adoption is shaky," she adds. Mrs. Lawrence is upset.

"People lie to us all the time," Elise says, hanging up the phone. "They have no idea that these lies have consequences for the animals." She calls the Volks to tell them that Pip is not six but eleven, letting them down softly. "He's very healthy and he came through the surgery in top shape," she explains. "We all thought he could easily have been six years old; he's so energetic." But the Volks want to reconsider the adoption. I am wondering how much they really want this dog. "If they pull out, we can't blame them," says Laura-Ann sympathetically. "They just watched their other springer die." Pip is lying on the floor sleeping, his usual mode. His tennis ball, which he never lets out of his sight, is tucked under his nose.

I walk into the office a day later and pick up the phone. It's the Volks, and they want to speak with Elise. She grabs the receiver and talks with them for several minutes. There's so much noise in the office that it's difficult to know what they are telling her. When she hangs up the phone, Elise slowly and dramatically walks to the microphone as if she's about to belt out a song. Then she turns on the mike and says over the loudspeaker: "Listen up, everybody. Pip is going home!"

Is IT POSSIBLE for a dog to act one way in a shelter and another way in a person's home? Absolutely. But when radically new behaviors are reported after only a short interval, the shelter staff is suspicious. Dogs, not unlike people, need time to adjust to their new surroundings. Some are quicker at this than others. Snowy, my own dog, was on her best behavior for two weeks before she felt relaxed enough to begin chewing through the house. A week after Pip goes to his new home, Mrs. Volk calls the shelter. She's very upset, but I can't exactly understand what has happened. Elise is not around, so I hang in. Finally I realize that she is telling me that she has a communication problem with Pip—the dog is deaf!

I'm wondering if Pip simply doesn't speak German. If Pip is deaf, he must be able to read lips. No one at the shelter suspected that he couldn't hear. But Mrs. Volk has another complaint. Pip tried to bite her and now she is frightened of him. While I'm on the phone with her, Mr. Volk walks in with the dog. "Here's your husband, right now," I say to her, surprised to see them. "Yes!" she shouts at me, in frustration. She has been trying to tell me over and over that he was on his way to the shelter. Welcome back, Pip.

Andrea comes running into the office to get Pip. "I can't understand how any human being could not love this dog," she says indignantly. The Volks are no longer looking like saints. Everyone glares at Mr. Volk as he does the requisite paperwork. "It wasn't a good placement. We're sorry," Laura-Ann tells him politely. To his credit, he doesn't ask for a refund.

Pip is put through a number of hearing tests, and everyone is startled to realize that he is a little deaf. But somehow this impairment makes the dog seem even more endearing. He is selected to be photographed for the local paper, accompanying Minky Johnson's regular shelter news column. Minky, now in her seventies, is a past president of the Humane Society board, an avid animal lover, and a local humanitarian. Her columns are packed with seasonal tips on how to care for pets, interspersed with letters, poems, and profiles of the available dogs and cats at the shelter. The animals photographed for her columns frequently get adopted. "If this doesn't do it, let's just make him our mascot and keep him in the office," suggests Dohrman. Everyone agrees.

But Pip's adventures aren't quite over. Just as the staff gets used to having him in the office, Marilyn Poole, a state employee who lives outside of Albany, sees his picture in the paper and clips it out. Every breed seems to have its share of followers; Marilyn and her husband, Tom, are springer spaniel people.

Marilyn decides to drive over to the shelter with her six-year-old daughter, Alyssa, to meet the dog. Marilyn is a warm, genial woman, gentle with the dog, and not the least bit put off by the application procedure. I like her immediately. Staff members rave to her so much about this old dog, one might think he was the reincarnation of Rin Tin Tin. But Marilyn takes the information in stride.

When I am outside alone with Mrs. Poole, trying to suss her out, I explain bluntly that Pip is eleven years old, just survived surgery, might have health problems, is almost deaf, and has been through at least two other homes that we know about. "If we don't find the right home, the shelter will probably keep him," I add. Marilyn just shakes her head in dismay and says, "Gee, what a great dog to go through all that."

Mrs. Poole wants to bring the whole family, including Gibbles, their current springer, back to the shelter to meet Pip. By the time she leaves, everyone is hoping that the family will take the dog.

Gibbles turns out to be a wonderfully spoiled, bubbly creature with an impeccably groomed coat. When Pip meets her, he is immediately attracted by her charms. The family decides on the spot to offer Pip a home.

A few days later, when Marilyn and her daughter come to pick up the dog, they arrive in a van with a bed in the back made up for Pip. The old dog hops into their car and lies right down as if he had been doing exactly that his entire life. Laura-Ann takes pictures of the dog before they leave, which I have never seen her do before. When they drive away, the director starts crying, uncontrollably. Somehow, Pip has pushed her over an emotional cliff, where saving one life only reminds her of those who have not been so lucky. "If they could all have homes like this one," Laura-Ann comments, blowing her nose.

After three days, when no one has heard from the Pooles, I want to call them to check up on the dog. "Don't bother them," advises Lori. "If they have a problem, you'll hear from them soon enough."

Laura-Ann disagrees. "Go ahead and call," she tells me. "If they do have a problem, maybe we can solve it before they bring the dog back."

I dial their number apprehensively, but Marilyn picks up right away and is so gracious that she puts me right at ease. She's pleased to hear from the shelter and apologetic for not having called earlier herself. "Now I know why all of you were so crazy about this dog," she says. She goes on and on about the new member of their family. "You don't have to worry anymore about Pip," Marilyn reassures me.

When I hang up to report the good news, everyone is relieved. They don't care about the details; all they want to know is that the dog is a keeper. Now they can let go of Pip and make room in a corner of their collective heart for the next dog in line who will need an extra push. Who will it be? Princess, the nervous cocker mix surrendered with behavior problems? Grover, the lovable husky who keeps running away from adopters? What about Marco Polo, the Great Dane mix who is going cage-crazy? What can be done for Smokey, the cranky terrier? Or Bandit, the hyper redbone coonhound? Could it be Sage, Honey Bear, Spike, Walt, Lancelot, Clyde, Gloria, Chewbacca, Cinnabar, Bouncer, Mitsi, Annie, Arthur, Bogart, Mystic, Hugo, Buster, Wishbone, Rufus, Madison, Zeplin, Chinook, Ms. Bowser, or Arlo?

THE EXPERIENCE WITH PIP inspires me to champion a dog who I feel has been given a bad rap. Buster, a purebred boxer who was originally surrendered with his sister, Samantha, has been returned. On his personality profile, his owner wrote, "destructive when left alone" and "too strong for young children." The word "aggressive" is circled on a list of adjectives. Buster is labeled a difficult dog despite his affability. Laura-Ann is reluctant to place any animal who might potentially threaten children. Buster's future is not looking bright.

"Look at Zack," I tell Laura-Ann. "He was accused of biting a little girl, and now he's living with two children. Even Pip was returned for aggression," I add. Laura-Ann hates to be lobbied about particular animals. She appreciates information about them but not pressure to save their lives. "Watch Buster for a week," she says, offering a compromise. "And get the dog assessed by a trainer."

Buster is not the kind of dog who ordinarily attracts me. Usually I go for the older, more soulful mongrels. Boxers are too muscular, and they don't have enough hair. This one's ears are docked so short they look like they were done at home on the kitchen table, and his big wet eyes bulge out of their sockets, making him look like a bug. But there is something so appealing about this dog's character that he is changing my opinion of the breed. When I bring Buster into the office, everyone, including Lori Beckers, is skeptical. But the dog proves me right. Buster has hidden reserves. He adjusts quickly to strangers, lying quietly in the office as people come and go. When I take him out for a walk, he turns out to be leash-trained. Buster starts to grow on everybody.

When a volunteer trainer shows up to check out a huge rottweiler, I ask her to look at Buster. She puts him on a lead and walks him a little, then she touches him all over his body, including his feet. She puts her hand right in his mouth. The dog seems very alert, thriving on the interaction. Then the woman backs away from Buster and calls him. The dog comes bounding over, jumps up, and licks her face. She grabs him and puts him down on his back. The dog just lies there waiting to have his belly scratched. Buster is either schizophrenic or a fabulous dog. "He's fine," the trainer says. "No, he's not fine—he's great." (The rottweiler was great, too, once he got outside of his cage.)

Laura-Ann asks me to find out what exactly went wrong in his previous home. When I call, I get a woman who says she is the niece of Buster's former owners, who are away on vacation. She tells me that Buster was out of control, running loose all day on their dairy farm.

"Where was he at night?" I ask.

"In a shed," she tells me.

"Alone?"

"Yes." There was another dog in the house who wasn't anxious to share his territory. Buster barked all night in the shed and frequently got out. When he started showing up at nearby houses, pawing at front doors, he became a nuisance. They brought him back to the shelter.

Many dogs do well on farms. Border collies, among other herding breeds, even have a genetic propensity to help out. But Buster wasn't suited to this placement. All he wanted was to be with people. Now I had real ammunition to place this dog.

I kept thinking about Samantha, Buster's sister. She had been placed with Terry and Mary Moon, a couple with four young children. I wondered if their boxer had demonstrated any behavior problems. "Go ahead and call them," says Laura-Ann.

I reach Terry Moon right away. He's a state trooper in Columbia County. "How's Samantha?" I ask tentatively.

"She's great," Terry says enthusiastically. "She's a member of the family, just like one of the children." Terry explains that they have become devotees of the breed. If Samantha could adjust well in a caring environment, then Buster deserved a chance to do the same.

When I mention to Terry that Samantha's brother is back in

the shelter, he says, "That dog has flashed through my mind a few times."

"Why don't you come see him," I suggest. "Wouldn't it be great to reunite the dogs?"

In less than twenty-four hours, Terry and Mary Moon arrive at the shelter—with Samantha. Buster is ecstatic at the reunion; his body ripples with delight. Samantha is friendly, too, but slightly cool. The Moons spend some time outside with both dogs. At the end of their visit, they come to the counter to tell the staff that they would like to offer Buster a home. The thrill is contagious.

I give the Moons a week with the dogs before I call to see how they are doing. If Pip can come back, any dog can. I am also concerned that a darker side of Buster might emerge. But when I reach Mary, she tells me Buster is thriving. Samantha, however, is a little overwhelmed by her brother.

Two weeks later, I arrive at their front door. They are my neighbors, and I can't resist the opportunity to see the dogs together. Buster is inside, eager to greet me. He's already gained several pounds and looks immeasurably healthier than the last time I saw him. Samantha is a little withdrawn. "She'll be fine," Mary tells me. "The dogs are great company for each other."

As I am leaving, both boxers greet one of the Moons' sons as he comes home from school. They don't jump all over him, but they do take turns licking his face before he can even put his backpack down. "The dogs are definitely ours," Mary tells me as we watch her son roll on the floor with Buster and Samantha. This is the kind of welcome-home greeting that children dream about.

———

I FINALLY DECIDE to take Lori Beckers up on her invitation to meet her animals. Lori has this crazy idea that I am going to adopt Ben, her rat, largely because she knows that my daughter, Kate, for reasons I don't fully comprehend, is enamored of rodents. I try to explain to Lori that there are already enough rats in New York City, but she insists that when I meet Ben, I'll change my tune.

The Beckerses live in a cozy cottage, just off the main drag that runs through Greenport. It's a suburban neighborhood. There's a little wooden wishing well in their front yard, along with two wooden piglets holding up a sign that says: THE BECKERS. When I arrive, Ben is outside in the yard sunning himself and munching on alfalfa in a large cage. Lori rushes out her front door, anxious to introduce me to the family. I decline the opportunity to hold Ben, in favor of meeting the rest of her relatives. "Hope you're ready for this," she says, as she opens her front door.

Much to my amazement, there are four large dogs hanging out contentedly, watching television in her living room. It's like a nursing home. Unlike Snowy, who barks hysterically when anyone comes over, this whole pack is quiet. "This is what old dogs are like," Lori tells me. The Beckers's house has no more than five hundred square feet of floor space. "My furniture is all in storage to make room for the dogs," she explains. There's a couch in the living room and a bed in the bedroom. That's it.

Cooper, an old black Labrador with a dusting of white around his mouth, is the first to greet me. The dog is twelve years old, and it is obvious at first glance that he is a saint. He was surrendered to the shelter at the age of nine. After he was placed, Lori swore that if he ever came back she would take him home herself. The dog was returned for allegedly nipping the children. "I never break my word to a dog," she says, winking.

"This one here's just about gone," Lori tells me when I ask about a massive hairy dog curled up in a corner of the room. Care Bear is a purebred Newfoundland that Paul took through a breed rescue group. He loves Newfies, as they are called, and he drove to Canada to pick this one up. "She's about twelve now, but she spent her last five years in a basement. The family got a new puppy and gave up on her," Lori explains. "When we first got her, she was completely bald. I spent four hundred dollars on vet bills getting her back into shape." Lori and Paul have had the dog for about two years. "She's got about a year left, but she doesn't know that. She's full of arthritis and lumps, but she's not in any pain. She sleeps well and eats well." Care Bear gets up to give me a friendly sniff and then goes back to her corner and lies down. "That's her spot," says Lori.

There is also a large collie mix in the room, a darker version of Lassie. The dog hangs back. She ducks when I reach to pat her head. "When I first brought Tasha home, she was very hand-shy. If you drop something on the ground, she still goes into a state of panic, waiting to be punished. So now when something drops, or there's a noise, I make a fun deal out of it and pat her a lot, like it's part of the everyday routine. She's getting better." Lori took Tasha home to foster her. The dog had been placed by the shelter at age ten and returned when her owner went on welfare a year later. The surrenderer wept at the counter; she had taken the best care of Tasha that she could afford. "I can't give Tasha up now," Lori explains. "She's made too much progress, and it would be traumatic for her to move again." Moreover, Lori loves her. Tasha is her shadow in the house.

Fluffy is a large seventy-pound longhaired mutt who is keeping her distance from me. "She's the newest one," explains Lori. "Fluffy was brought to the shelter about a month ago for euthanasia. She was a mess, had a big tumor on her back. Well, we got rid of that, didn't we, old girl?" she says in a baby voice, looking right at the dog. Fluffy comes running over and buries her nose in Lori's lap. "She's going to be just fine," she continues, as she shows me the scar where the tumor came off.

"OK. Are you ready for this?" Lori asks. "It's time for Kipper to come in." Kipper, number five, is out in the yard. His arrival cannot go unnoticed; he's a huge red dog who thinks the world is his oyster. He comes bounding in, seeming to fill every inch of available space, jumping up and nuzzling us and all the dogs as well. Even Care Bear seems to like him. Kipper has much more energy than the rest.

Then I realize that Kipper is, or was, Nevada, the oversized golden retriever who came in with health problems, dragging a chain around his neck. But this dog looks young and silky. "Is that Nevada?" I ask incredulously.

"You bet," says Lori. The dog's transformation is remarkable. "I thought he was an old, pathetic dog with skin problems who didn't have a chance of getting adopted," she explains. "So I took him home and put him on a good diet. Turns out he was just a little depressed. Kipper's seven years old and acts like an overgrown puppy. Eats everything in sight. Stole a cucumber off the counter last night. He's the youngster in my group." She laughs and rubs the dog's backside. They also recently discovered that he is diabetic. Either Lori or Paul gives him an injection every morning.

"Wait till you meet Arnold," Lori says, giving me a devilish grin. Then she shouts: "Hey, Arnie! You've got company, hon!"

There's a snorting sound from a little room off the kitchen, and out struts a creature that looks like a giant Brillo pad. This is the first Vietnamese potbellied pig I've ever met, eye-to-eye. Somehow I get the feeling I am the first writer he's ever met, up close. We're staring at each other, speechless. Arnie is Spielberg material; he looks cute and prehistoric. I don't know if he's going to charge at me or lick my hand like a dog.

"He's going to act real funny because there's a stranger in the house," says Lori. "Don't worry though, just say hello to him and give him a biscuit." Lori hands me a dog biscuit. "He'll eat anything," she says. I feed him the treat carefully, but he's still snorting at me through his little snout and looking at me as if I were an intruder. Lori insists that I touch him, so I pat his skin, which is rough and wiry, part-elephant, part-porcupine. "His skin is dry and flaky, so I have to spray him down with lanolin and water," she explains. "He screams and hollers like heck when I do it. He hates getting wet."

I'm not sure why people are attracted to these pigs, although I am told they are adorable piglets, intelligent, and easy to housebreak. Lori is totally in love. She strokes Arnie affectionately and chats him up in a high-pitched voice. The pig responds to her every word and slowly backs off, retreating to his room off the kitchen.

"Arnie's got the run of the place," Lori tells me. "He goes in and out, using the yard with the dogs, and loves to watch television with me at night. He's four years old now, and they only live to be about nine."

"I thought Vietnamese pigs were small."

"You see? That's what happens when people don't really know what they're getting into," Lori says, recognizing that she has a pig novice in her home. "Arnie is mixed with farm hog, but the people who bought him didn't realize it. They were told he was going to be about fifty pounds. I've never seen one less than sixty or seventy pounds." I'm suddenly remembering the woman who brought home a baby pig to her New York City apartment. The pig grew so large that the woman couldn't get him out her front door; he was eventually taken out the window by a piano mover.

"I could not be happy without a pig," Lori says matter-of-factly. She got Arnie through Pigs, A Sanctuary, a rescue organization in Charleston, West Virginia. When her previous pig died, Lori contacted the group and they sent her to Long Island to pick up Arnie, who had literally outgrown his welcome.

"Does Arnie play with the dogs?" I ask.

"No. The dogs stay clear of him. Arnie is the boss, and he has his own room." We walk into a little alcove near the back door. There's a nest of blankets and pillows on the floor. On one wall, there's a glass case that holds Lori's collection of 250 glass and ceramic pigs. On the opposite side of the room, there's a glass tank containing a pool of water, some rocks, and a large green iguana eating a mound of wet dog food. "Surprise!" says Lori. "This is Iggy. We've had him since he was tiny. Want to hold him?"

"Don't disturb him, he's eating," I beg her. Iggy is two feet long and looks like he weighs at least ten pounds. "This is the only pet

Paul and I ever bought," she concedes. They got him at a pet store. Just couldn't resist.

All but Iggy are shelter saves. Lori's mutts have been through home after home, but their last time through the shelter they would not have made it out alive. "It really hurts me when people say they don't want to take home an older dog because they won't fit into their households or they're too old to be trained," she says. "Look at my dogs. Older dogs make great pets. They're calm and grateful when you take them home. These dogs all walked into my house and were immediately comfortable." They are an exceptional group of well-mannered, amiable creatures. "They know exactly why they're here," she adds. "Everybody gets along with everybody else because there's just nowhere else to go."

Hilary and Lady,
surrendered
for refusing to
hunt rabbits

FOUR

Difficult Dogs, Difficult People

As THE WEATHER TURNS COLD, the end-of-summer del
uge of garden-variety dogs and cats—not to mention rabbits, ferrets, hamsters, goats, iguanas, birds (including twenty finches
from a bankrupt breeder, who are placed in a nursing home)—
floods the shelter. Late August and September are the cruelest
months of sheltering in upstate New York. The summer people are
heading back to the city, and children are starting school, which
means their dogs and cats are about to become very inconvenient.
The tourists are going home. Hack horses at riding camps who
carried people up and down mountain trails will be shipped off to
auction where they are likely to be sold by the pound for slaughter.
There are no children left to pat the animals in petting zoos or visit

the bears at the Catskill Game Farm. Some of these hardworking animals will make it through the winter, while others will be destroyed simply because it is more cost-effective than feeding and sheltering them until next summer.

The shelter is swamped with animals who are being given up by their owners or left behind. A ten-year-old girl brings in a flea-infested puppy that her mother won't let her keep beyond summer vacation; two beagles, sisters named Hilary and Lady, are dumped because they refuse to hunt rabbits; a landlord brings in a red collie mix abandoned in a summer rental. A young man shows up with two "stray" pit bulls who are covered with scars. A black Lab is surrendered when his owner is arrested on drug charges, not to mention suspicion of murdering his wife, whose body turned up floating in the Hudson River. The dog is a nervous wreck, but alive at least.

As the abandoned animals fill the shelter, brought in either by dog-control officers or neighbors who couldn't stand to hear cats crying for food any longer, I remember Laura-Ann's prediction that I would eventually become more sympathetic with the animals than their owners. It is impossible not to resent those who discard their pets as easily as their old clothes. And I do, especially when the animals come in abused. Chances are, when a crazy dog arrives at the shelter, there's a crazy person at the other end of the leash.

Dogs are born with more or less intelligence, but there's no gene for an abused personality. Shelter workers must be able to distinguish abused dogs from well-socialized ones and aggressive dogs from frightened ones. Surrenderers frequently tell the shelter that the dog they are giving up is aggressive because that's a good reason to get rid of one. But many of these dogs are only acting defensively, trying to protect themselves from their owners. They have learned from experience to cringe at the sight of a hand or stick. (Snowy was initially afraid of boots because she had been kicked.) Distinguishing an aggressive dog from an abused one is not easy; sometimes there's too thin a line between them and the distinction becomes moot. The dog cannot—and maybe should not—be saved.

One of the first indications that a dog might be in trouble is a troublesome owner. There are several notorious individuals in the community who surrender animal after animal in rough shape. Only the dogs seem to get rehabilitated. Their owners remain unchanged. "I have another complaint on April King," Laura-Ann tells the staff. "Big surprise," chimes in Lori Beckers.

"Who is she?" I ask. Laura-Ann disappears into her office and comes back with a file. "Read it," she says, "so I don't have to tell you the story."

The file contains a surrender sheet for a deceased black cat, dated May 15, 1994. Under "Reason for surrender," April wrote in awkward print: "Husband killed cat." April turned her husband in to the police and called the Humane Society. The file also includes a copy of her deposition to the Hudson Police Department, which describes Arthur King taking their cat into the bathroom and slitting his throat with a knife. "I started hearing the cat crying real loud and then after a few seconds it quieted down to nothing," April reported to the officer.

Arthur was arrested and eventually sentenced to three months' probation. He never served any jail time or paid any fines. His wife, however, left him.

The cat murder turned April into a celebrity, of sorts, at the shelter. Unfortunately, Arthur was not the only problem in the family. April, too, made it onto the Warning List as she began bringing animal after animal to the shelter, all of whom were in sorry shape. "You've met her," Laura-Ann says to me. "Didn't you take China in at the counter?"

I suddenly remember April King. She's about thirty years old, a little overweight, and appeared emotionally off balance. She was also memorable because she spoke in such an inappropriately disparaging way about her dog, a humble Labrador mix. China, originally named Lady, was seven months old, not housebroken, and shaking with fear. She was thin, infested with worms. The dog had been beaten around her face. She was exceedingly hand-shy, withdrawn around people, and failed to respond to her own name. I promptly gave her a fresh identity. The dog was fragile, like a china doll, hence her new name.

China refused to come forward in her cage without a great deal of coaxing. Nevertheless, she wasn't aggressive, and as she began to realize that the shelter was a safe place, she slowly started to interact with people. China sat in the main kennel for weeks, however, because there were so many similar black dogs who were more outgoing and responsive. For three months, I watched people pass over this quiet dog, until finally a woman named Beverly Kipp walked through the kennel and made an immediate connection. The Kipps' dog had recently died, and they were searching for another. They adopted China, who was renamed Molly, taken to obedience training, housebroken, and successfully integrated into the family's life. It is tremendously gratifying when abused dogs successfully move on to good homes.

Now Laura-Ann has received an anonymous tip from a friend who saw King on the street kicking a puppy. Her source is willing to put her name on a complaint if the shelter will go in and investigate. "But we can't just go in and take her puppy, unless, of course, the dog is in really bad shape," the director reminds me. "We have to work within the law." She picks up the phone and calls DeLisle to discuss the case. "Not *her* again," he comments. "I'll be right over."

The last humane officer to visit King was Tom LaBuda, who convinced her to surrender two Border collie puppies, one of whom, Mickey, had a fractured hip. A witness had seen her throw the pup down on a cement sidewalk, which is when he got hurt. King swiftly gave up both puppies to avoid arrest. Soon after, they were adopted. Mickey required a seven-hundred-dollar operation. Today the dog walks with a permanent limp, but his new owner is devoted.

When DeLisle arrives, he and Laura-Ann debate the legal implications of seizing another King puppy. Laura-Ann wants the dog out, if possible, before King does more damage. "If it were anyone else, I wouldn't rush over," says Lee. "We need to get her into court with an animal in very bad shape." This is the only way to put an animal abuser out of business altogether.

In certain states, King would not be allowed to go through dog after dog. The Humane Society could take her to court and make sure she never got her hands on another animal. Lee shows me a copy of a signed affidavit from a cruelty case in Cheyenne, Wyoming. A woman named Terri Smith pled guilty to "one count of failing to provide nine puppies (and a female) with sufficient food and water," on September 2, 1992. The judge slapped her with the maximum fine and sentence, $520 and six months in jail. He then suspended the jail sentence, telling her, "You will not be allowed to own any animals. You will not be allowed to borrow or possess any animals. You will not be allowed to work anywhere that animals are kept. You will not be allowed to have contact with any animals for the rest of your life. If you do, you will have to serve the maximum sentence that I can give—six months in the county jail."

This kind of opinion, circulated throughout humane societies, makes cruelty officers salivate. But the language of the decision went even further, beyond anyone's wildest expectations. The judge authorized the Laramie County Sheriff's Department, with the approval of the district attorney's office, "to enter and search [Mrs. Smith's] premises at any time without [her] consent and if any animals are found, they are to be immediately confiscated and [Mrs. Smith is] to be immediately arrested to begin serving six months in jail."

DeLisle, unfortunately, is working in New York State, where the judges rarely hand out severe sentences to animal abusers. In Columbia and Greene Counties, the local district attorneys do not consider the average cruelty a priority, let alone a crime worthy of severe financial penalties or jail time. Animals can sit in cages for months or years, held as evidence for cases that the courts seem loath to consider. Repeat offenders are the rule, not the exception. "We're at the bottom of the criminal justice dung pile," explains Lee. A similar situation faces investigators all over the country.

Lee and I pack the van with a dog crate and head over to April King's apartment. Ten minutes later we are ringing her doorbell, with no idea what we are going to find inside. When April opens the door, her jaw drops at the sight of Officer DeLisle. King knows precisely why he is paying her a visit.

"May we come in?" Lee asks politely. He introduces me to April, who nods her head and opens the door for us to enter. She looks like she is going to burst into tears. The apartment is filled with smoke and the smell of meat; King's boyfriend, whom I also recognize from the day I met China, is cooking hamburgers for dinner. The two of them are living in a one-room apartment on the first floor of a small building in Hudson. The place looks out onto a wide street where cars are zooming past the window.

The apartment is furnished sparingly and is quite neat. There's a puppy sitting near a twenty-pound bag of generic Wal-Mart dog food; a full bowl of kibble is waiting for her, untouched. Part of the floor is covered with newspaper and a few chew toys are scattered about. The dog, a black-and-white hound mix, looks to be about ten weeks old. She comes toward us slowly; she's shy, but playful.

"Where did you get her?" asks Lee, breaking the tension.

"From a woman handing out pups in the parking lot of Price Chopper," she says.

Lee bends down to pat the dog on her head, and then he rubs his hands over her rib cage.

"You're not getting this one," April blurts out angrily. "I'm not going to let you take this one away." Then she begins to whimper. "I love this puppy. I won't hurt her. I promise I won't. This time it's going to be different." How different can it possibly be this time around?

"I've already got a report at the shelter," Lee continues. "You were seen dragging this puppy along the street, kicking her, and screaming your head off at the dog. The puppy was crying and scared, April."

"I'm just trying to train her to walk on a leash. I won't do nothing to this puppy. I swear, I won't. I love her." April scoops the pup up off the floor and hugs her tightly. She's protecting the puppy from Lee, as if he were going to snatch the dog out of her arms and run. April kisses the little dog over and over with her eyes closed.

Lee is looking very uncomfortable. Yet he wants the dog. I don't say a word.

"April, are you really able to take care of a pet? Think about it," he says, trying a new approach. "Dogs are so much work. They're a real pain, and they're expensive. Why don't you just surrender the puppy to me right now, and neither of us will worry about the complaint I have on my desk."

"No way," she fires back at him. "You're not taking my dog. I know you can't do it legally."

Lee pauses. He's surprised she knows the law. Indeed, he can't just seize the dog; she looks fine. "Have you taken the puppy to a vet to get her first shots?"

"Not yet, but I have an appointment. I just called."

Lee looks at me. I'm on the floor with the puppy. She's a little thin, and her coat is flaky and dry, but the law doesn't allow the Humane Society to take dogs from their owners because they're on poor diets and have dandruff.

"Look, April. We're going to leave. But if I get one more report that you're hurting this little dog, I won't just come and take this puppy, I will get a warrant for your arrest. Do you understand?"

April nods. Her boyfriend is staring at us while their dinner is burning.

"So you remember: We will be watching you day and night. If you hurt this dog again, I'll know about it." Lee goes for the door, and I follow. It slams closed behind us.

There is something clearly wrong with April King. Just the way she holds her body and speaks makes it apparent that she is a barely functional person; her eyes wander, and she is disheveled, as if she might have trouble dressing herself. She participates in county programs for the developmentally disabled but seems to live for her animals. Whether this need is a result of her emotional problems or in spite of them is not clear. Either way, April searches out the company of animals and then, apparently, beats them.

April and her new boyfriend, who has a car, have been frequent visitors to the shelter, where April dreams about bringing more animals home. The day she dropped off China, she inquired about putting in an application to adopt Patch, a lively dalmatian-mix puppy. Laura-Ann kindly explained that Patch already had a home. It was a white lie. She could have simply refused April the dog and told her never to come back. The reason she didn't, however, is that the director wants April to feel comfortable at the shelter so she will continue to voluntarily bring in her animals when she can no longer cope with them.

Having a pet around might ease April's anxieties and make her feel more connected to reality. But should she be allowed to have one? "If it were up to the Humane Society, absolutely not," Lee tells me. "But in New York State, April certainly has the legal right to a pet. I just wish she'd try goldfish."

Shelter workers meet numerous borderline psychotics bringing in nervous—very nervous—dogs. These are people who "love" animals but cannot possibly care for them. Whether or not they have the ability to care for themselves, or their children, is also questionable. The last straw, which often leads them to a shelter, is a health problem or a landlord dispute; when their pets start to get sick, become prohibitively expensive to maintain, or are too disruptive, they are brought to the shelter. These are the clients that veterinarians rarely see, unless they reach out to the community. Their owners generally can't afford regular vaccinations or any care at all for their animals. It's as if veterinarians and shelter workers serve two different populations of animal owners. Vets largely work with clients who pamper their pets, while shelters deal with people who neglect theirs. Many of them are homeless, or about to slip through the holes of whatever safety nets are still in place. No statistics are kept on how many adult animals, especially cats, arrive at Columbia-Greene never having seen the inside of a veterinarian's office. But there are many.

I learn to identify potentially difficult people right away, just as I learn to identify their difficult dogs.

When Mrs. Taylor bangs on the shelter door with her cane at the end of a long day, I know immediately that something is wrong. "The dog was supposed to stay with a man in Greene County, but he's not there," she says to me, as if we were in the middle of a conversation that has been interrupted. "Don't know where he is. But I can't keep the dog. Won't do it any longer." The woman rambles on and then begins complaining about her daughter, who just went into the hospital again, this time for knee surgery. An ambulance had to pick her up. The daughter left behind two children and a brown dog named Windy, who looks like a dingo. Mrs. Taylor is accompanied by her granddaughter, Becky; Windy is waiting nervously in the car.

"One of the girls had to be sent away," she says. "What kind of mother can't take care of her own children? Becky is difficult enough, but I can't control the dog at all." The child, about eight years old, is listening, her eyes glued to the floor. She's a pretty, blond-haired girl with a loose braid falling down her back. When I smile at her, she looks away.

"My daughter doesn't know I'm doing this," Mrs. Taylor comments as she signs the form to surrender Windy. "I promised her I'd take care of this dog, but I just can't do it. She pulls so hard on the leash my back is aching, and when I tie her up, she gets away." Windy is four years old. She has been running from these people for years. "She's a good dog," Mrs. Taylor adds. "You won't hurt her, will you?"

As usual, I try to be reassuring, an ability that I am learning to perfect. The shelter tries to encourage people to feel positive about their decision to give up an animal. But there is no comforting Mrs. Taylor. She wants to linger and complain about how hard her life is, how little money she has, and how much she doesn't want this dog. "No one ever helps me," she says gloomily. Actually, I'm trying to help her. I suggest several times that giving up this dog might enable her to focus more on her family, which is where she is needed, but Mrs. Taylor has absolutely no interest in anything I have to say. It's as if I am talking to someone who is not there. The little girl is catatonic.

When the phone rings, I go to pick it up, hoping Mrs. Taylor will see I'm busy and just leave. It's Laura-Ann calling me from inside her office. "Tell her she has to leave," the director says. "Be forceful or she'll be here all night."

"Come on out and help me," I whisper. "I can't get rid of her. I have no authority. I'm just a volunteer, remember?"

"You *can* get rid of her," Laura-Ann says. "Use me as your last resort." I decide to give it one more try. I take a deep breath and return to the counter. I explain that the shelter is closing and it's time for her to go. For a moment, Mrs. Taylor and I seem to be speaking the same language, and she reluctantly prepares to leave. "My daughter's going to be very upset. Don't call her right away," she begs me. "She's going to kill me, you know." She repeats this prediction with such gravity in her voice that I begin to think it might be true. For her, turning in this dog is a dangerous act of betrayal. I remember when my parents gave away my dog, a schnauzer named Winston, one summer while I was at camp. I wanted to kill them! I do not share this anecdote with Mrs. Taylor.

The woman finally leaves, and Laura-Ann comes out of hiding with Dohrman, who has been working in the director's office. Always practical, Dohrman locks the front door. Laura-Ann has been on the phone with the dog-control officer responsible for Philmont (hometown of Oliver North), where Mrs. Taylor lives. Windy has been a problem for months. "The family isn't taking proper care of her," says Laura-Ann. "It's a good thing we have her." I'm starting to feel better about this betrayal.

But before our conversation is finished, Mrs. Taylor reappears, banging on the door, once again, with her cane. I can't believe it. Laura-Ann retreats to her office. "You have to stay," I plead. "Tell her we're closed for the day—no more transactions," she says, leaving. "I'm here," says Dohrman, going back to her own desk. At least she's in the room.

I realize that Mrs. Taylor must have driven her car to the end of the road, made a U-turn, and come right back. As I open the door, she hobbles in with her cane. Becky is still by her side. "I've changed my mind," she says. "I want the dog back."

"But you just spent an hour telling me that you are unable to take care of Windy."

"I want her back. I've changed my mind. My daughter's going to kill me. I just can't do it. Windy's a good dog." The woman speaks in short, crisp sentences.

"If Windy's a good dog, why don't you do the right thing for her? She's in a kennel with a blanket and big bowl of food. Nothing is going to happen to the dog tonight. Look, I'm just a volunteer," I add. "Sleep on your decision, and call the director in the morning."

Regardless of my assurances, Mrs. Taylor simply stands at the counter and insists, over and over, that I go fetch her dog. The more I refuse, the more frantic she becomes. The easiest thing to do would be to just give her the damn dog and get rid of her, which is tempting. But I realize that there's no chance Laura-Ann is going to give this woman the dog tonight, or possibly ever. All the shelter's strict adoption policies are starting to make sense. I realize that my mission is to protect this dog. Now I'm wondering if the Humane Society can keep Becky, too.

"I want the dog back—now!" She starts shouting at me. "Who the hell do you think you are? It's my dog. Where is she anyway?" Then Mrs. Taylor marches into the kennel searching for Windy.

The dogs were lying quietly in their cages, but now they go off in unison like a burglar alarm. "You can't go in there!" I shout, dragging her out of the kennel. "Besides, Windy isn't in there. Sit down, please. Let me get the director."

I go into Laura-Ann's office and close the door; Dohrman is watching Mrs. Taylor. Laura-Ann is sitting at her desk with her head in her hands, having overheard the whole ordeal.

"What are you going to do?" I ask.

"You mean, 'What are *we* going to do?'" she responds. Then she says with determination, "We're going to get her out of here— without the dog." Before we go back into the war zone, Laura-Ann picks up the phone and beeps Dohrman, still sitting at her desk, and asks her to go out to the barn and get Lee DeLisle, who happens to be there checking on some horses.

"Maybe Lee should bring Lucas in with him," I suggest, as a joke, referring to a formidable rottweiler in the kennel. "Lee won't need Lucas," responds Laura-Ann.

As we walk into the room, I hear Mrs. Taylor saying, "Don't worry, Becky. We'll get Mommy's dog back." Laura-Ann grabs Windy's paperwork, gives it a once-over, and asks, "What's the problem, Mrs. Taylor? You asked us to take in your dog, and we're glad to. Windy will get good care here."

"I want her back. I've changed my mind. It's my daughter's dog. I promised I wouldn't bring her here."

Laura-Ann is direct—always the best policy. "I'm not going to release the dog to you tonight. The shelter is closed. You've signed the paperwork, and I'm legally responsible for Windy now. We can talk this over tomorrow. I'd like to speak to your daughter directly and see if she can make alternate plans for the dog. But Windy is going to stay in our custody tonight."

"I'll call the police," the irate grandmother threatens.

"Please do," says Laura-Ann calmly. "You can use my phone."

Mrs. Taylor is about to have a meltdown. She pounds her cane on the floor twice, sits down in a chair, and says, "I'm not leaving until you give me my dog. Becky, you sit right here with me." She grabs the little girl, using her as a kind of shield.

"Mrs. Taylor, if you don't leave right now, I'm going to call the police myself and have you arrested for trespassing. This is a private facility, and I am ordering you to get off the property." Then Laura Ann walks to the other side of the counter and takes the woman's arm to escort her out the door.

"Don't you touch me!" Mrs. Taylor screams, giving Laura-Ann a hard whop on the arm with her cane. "Call the sheriff," Laura-Ann yells to me. "Tell them I've been assaulted by someone who will not leave the premises!"

I pick up the phone and call the emergency number that is pasted to the desk on a red sticker. The officer who answers the phone is immediately responsive. "We're minutes away," he says. "There's a car out in Claverack." Everyone knows where the shelter is located.

"They're on their way," I tell Laura-Ann, who is standing close to Mrs. Taylor, guarding her prisoner like a Doberman. Mrs. Taylor is about a foot taller than Laura-Ann and twice her weight.

When Lee walks in, his presence seems to calm everything down, at least initially. "I just called the police," Laura-Ann informs him. "Mrs. Taylor struck me with her cane and is refusing to leave the shelter." Her arm has a red welt on it. Mrs. Taylor is silent, but then she abruptly goes for the door in an attempt to make a fast exit. "You're not going anywhere until the police get here," Lee tells her sharply. "Sit down."

But much to my amazement, Taylor tries to push Lee aside and bolt again. The woman is in her sixties; Lee is a large man. He grabs her and twists her arms behind her back. "Get my handcuffs," he calls to me. I run over to his desk and fish a pair of shiny handcuffs out of his briefcase. As I hand Lee the cuffs, Becky bursts into tears and runs outside. "What kind of example are you setting for your little girl?" Lee asks her. "Would you like her to watch me handcuff you to the chair, Mrs. Taylor?" The woman finally decides to sit down just as two police cars pull into the parking lot.

While the police interrogate Mrs. Taylor and Cammisa, I go outside to find Becky, who is sitting in her grandmother's car. The child looks at me for the first time and says, "Don't hurt my grandmother. She's just trying to help my mom." I promise that her grandmother will not get hurt. "But she can't go around hitting people with her cane," I say. She raises her head and nods. I wonder if she knows the sting of that cane, too.

When Mrs. Taylor finally emerges from the shelter, she has been issued a summons, which means she must get a lawyer and show up at a hearing. Laura-Ann has decided to press charges. I have mixed feelings about dragging this irrational woman into court. "I can't let anyone get away with this kind of behavior in the shelter," the director says to me.

The next morning Laura-Ann tracks down Karen Taylor at a hospital in Pittsfield. The daughter, unlike her mother, is easy to talk to. She is grateful that her dog is safe and in the shelter. When

Karen agrees to allow Laura-Ann to spay Windy, the director becomes more sympathetic to her plight and decides to board the dog for two weeks, at a minimum fee. By then, Karen will be out of the hospital and able to pick up Windy herself; her mother is banned from the shelter. "I'll give you two weeks, exactly," Laura-Ann repeats. "Then I'm going to adopt her out."

Windy is so nervous her first few days that the kennel staff wants to let her settle before sending her off to be spayed. The dog backs away from people, doesn't eat well, and walks back and forth in her kennel like a stir-crazy lion in a zoo. The problem, however, is not the cage. When the dog is outside, she is equally anxious, pulling so hard at the end of her leash that she continually chokes herself and gags. Laura-Ann takes a special interest in Windy, but she can barely control her. Windy is in worse shape than many others. She is not aggressive, but she lives in a state of fear. Day by day, little by little, she warms up to the staff.

Karen shows up on day fourteen to pick up her dog. The staff is very unhappy to see Windy returned to her owner. "It's her dog," says Laura-Ann, defending her decision. "We have no cause to keep her."

Sometimes I wonder why people want dogs at all. Cats are easier to keep; dogs require so much care. They are not as demanding as children, but close to it. Actually, children are the ones who usually ask for a dog. I watch family after family come to the shelter because the kids want a pet. Parents will even admit that they dread the event. "I don't want to do this, but Henry insists," one mother told me, as she filled out an application on a puppy. Henry was six. His main criterion was that the pup had to look like Scooby-Doo, his favorite cartoon character.

Thanks to the kids, one shelter in Florida received a 35 percent increase in dalmatians after *101 Dalmatians* hit theaters. Most dalmatians, ironically, do not make it back out again because they are surrendered for being aggressive toward children. Any shelter worker will tell you that, contrary to popular opinion, young children (under eight) and animals do not mix. The cats get thrown in the tub to see if they can swim, and the puppies get kicked around like footballs; all of them get their tails pulled, eyes poked, and necks nearly broken, until they learn to respond defensively or, when possible, hide. Inevitably, the dogs start nipping and the cats start scratching, all having learned to dislike little people. Suddenly, Ginger and Tiger aren't looking so adorable anymore. Reluctantly, mom or dad takes them to the shelter because they have more important things to worry about than the safety of the children in their own homes. Kids should have stuffed animals that can be squeezed to death, not real ones.

The volume of animals turned in to this little shelter is mind-numbing. I start to understand why Cammisa screens people so carefully. I find myself spending more time talking people out of adopting animals than into taking them home. They either have too many children, select an inappropriate animal, or want a trophy dog to lie majestically on their front lawns—tied up, of course. Having a large purebred—usually a German shepherd, husky, or rottweiler (Dobermans seem to be out of fashion)—signifies a certain affluence and power to the neighbors. Denying people a dog simply because they intend to chain it to a tree is controversial; there may not be a law against keeping dogs outside, but there is a shelter policy against giving them to people who do it. "I can't stop people from tying up their dogs outside," says Laura-Ann, "but I can stop them from tying *our* dogs outside."

The goal is to get potential adopters to be honest about how they intend to contain their new pals.

Jeff Miller, no more than twenty-five, pulls up in a sparkling red Toyota truck. He's wearing a sleeveless shirt to show off his muscles and a tattoo of a military insignia on one of his arms. He wants to know if there are any "big rottweilers" in the kennel.

"They make great guard dogs, don't they," I say.

"Sure do," he says. "I've been looking for a good rottie for months."

"That makes sense," I tell him. "A Chihuahua would blow away in the back of that truck." We both laugh. Now I've got him, and I open up a conversation about animals he has loved. When people tell you their dog stories, they often narrate the passages of their own lives. This guy was born in Catskill, just across the river, and has had a parade of huskies, Labs, pit bulls, and girlfriends ever since. He's gotten rid of the dogs and the girls in the usual failure-to-commit syndrome. But the best dog he ever owned was a rottie named Robot who lasted eight years without getting into any trouble.

"They're really good about being chained up," I comment.

"The best," he says.

"What happened to Robot?"

"Got hit by a car," he tells me. "The dog broke his chain one night and ran into the road."

"You've got to bring them in at night, at least," I tell him. Jeff agrees. He was out of town, naturally, when the dog died.

Lucas, the current rottie, is sitting in the shelter, and I know this guy is going to want him bad, which he does. Miller fills out an application for the dog and tells an adoption counselor that Lucas will be with him all day and inside at night; he even wants to sign him up for a training class.

After Miller leaves I check out his application. The slot where he was suppose to list previous pets is blank. He has failed to mention the huskies, Labs, and pit bulls, for some reason. He also claims he has no local veterinarian, which is odd since he grew up in Catskill. When the shelter calls his landlord, he turns out to be Jeff's father, who confirms that his son has had numerous dogs. Moreover, his parents have no intention of allowing him to bring another, especially a large rottweiler, into their house. This will be an easy denial. Lucas will not be riding around in the back of Jeff's truck. Veterinarians spend a lot of time in Columbia County treating dogs who have fallen out of trucks and broken their legs, if not their necks. (In California, it is illegal to put a dog in the back of a pickup unless the animal is crated or cross-tethered.)

I begin to realize that if every person looking for a dog at the Columbia-Greene Humane Society took one home the same day, the surrenderers and the adopters would simply go round and round in a revolving door, trading animals. And the animals would get very dizzy.

"THERE IS NO such thing as a difficult dog, only an inexperienced owner," wrote the trainer Barbara Woodhouse in her book *No Bad Dogs*. She was understating the case. "Every once in a while I come across a dog that's just too far gone," says Cathy Crawmer, an animal behaviorist and trainer, currently working with adopters from the shelter, which tries to get as many new pet owners as possible into her class. Crawmer can make the difference for unruly dogs or puppies; well-behaved canines do not bounce back to the shelter. Most people, however, especially if they grew up with pets, don't feel they need a degree from a dog school. The shelter pushes training as a form of recreation, but it cannot disguise the problem that classes are time-consuming as well as expensive. Many people don't have the patience or extra income.

Crawmer's courses are worth every cent of the $125 fee for eight classes. Most trainers specialize in one species or another, but Crawmer's knowledge of all kinds of beasts is extensive. She has taught canaries how to sing and dogs how to ring doorbells. She has also dealt with the behavioral problems of lions and tigers, among other predators in zoos and circuses. Her work with some of the wilder animals has had an impact on the techniques she has developed to train dogs and cats. Crawmer's current goal is to reinvent the way people communicate with their pets, which might help keep thousands of animals from ending up in shelters.

Crawmer believes that most people do not understand how dogs think. Her theory is that if dogs knew what we wanted them to do, most of them would do it. But dogs don't respond to the kinds of corrections most people use, a whack on the snout or the backside. It's a vicious circle; people discipline their dogs, but nothing changes. If anything, the dog just gets worse. "Discipline equals abuse," says Crawmer. "The dog begins to assume you're a monster and starts developing bad habits. We bite our nails when we get nervous or anxious. Well, dogs start chewing, too."

In her class, Crawmer tries to get people to think about how *they* appear to their dogs, rather than the reverse. "*Dogs* can't be trained to read our minds," she tells her students, "but *we* can be trained to figure out what they're thinking." She explains that dogs who are out of control have not been given clear signals from their owners. "Dogs understand body language first, and words second," she says. Both have to be working in tandem. "Dogs aren't stupid, but they're simple," she states. To demonstrate this point, she does a hilarious rendition of how not to speak to a dog. First, she bends way over and starts begging a chocolate Lab, who happens to be sitting a few feet away, to please come over; the dog lifts up his head for a millisecond and then ignores her. Next, the trainer stands up straight, looks right at the dog, and in a firm voice says one word: "Come!" The Lab gets right up and walks over to her! "This is not a trick dog," says Crawmer, chuckling. She rewards the Lab immediately with a treat, a bit of Oinker Roll, a product made specially for dogs. Crawmer always trains with food rewards and positive reinforcement instead of traditional "discipline," which generally means punishment.

Crawmer is also highly regarded as an expert in agility, the fastest growing dog sport in the country. Agility is so popular upstate that there aren't enough teachers and classes to accommodate the demand. In agility, the dogs learn to run courses on command, weaving through poles, crawling through tunnels, and jumping over barriers. When Crawmer works her own dogs (pit bulls, Chihuahuas, and toy poodles), she sometimes allows Annie, her pygmy goat, trained with the dogs, to join them. At this point, she could probably train any species; even her pet fish jump through a hoop on command. They are rewarded with a treat, just like the dogs.

Bringing a trainer into a shelter can make a significant difference. Adopters like to walk in and meet a dog who already knows

how to walk on a leash, sit, and shake hands. If a dog offers someone a paw, the assumption is that the dog is smart and loves
people. Teaching a dog to sit and shake hands can take less than fifteen minutes—if the teacher is smart. In fact, just fifteen minutes
of training a day, if it is done correctly, can turn a problem dog
into a more appealing pet in a few weeks.

Unlike Woodhouse, Crawmer might suggest that "difficult"
owners create "inexperienced" dogs. Crawmer believes in nurture,
not nature, when it comes to dominant breeds like German shepherds and rottweilers. She is a passionate defender of pit bulls,
whom she believes have gotten an undeserved bad reputation, particularly in the press. "Dogs are not born with moral attitudes,"
she argues. "People have to point them in a particular direction."

Working with her friends Cydney Cross and Mary Allen, who
rescue local pit bulls, Crawmer turns them, as well as other allegedly "bad" dogs, into pussycats. Her best tool for correction,
believe it or not, is a simple spray bottle filled with water. Dogs and
cats hate being sprayed in their faces and will stop a multitude of
behaviors to avoid this irritant. In Crawmer's classes, everyone carries a spray bottle. Owners are instructed never to hit their dogs.
"You are the person who offers comfort when they are upset, not
abuse," she says repeatedly.

Charlene Marchand, president of the shelter board, is a trainer
and professional German shepherd breeder, who has worked for
years with Crawmer. Marchand's goal is to train the kennel staff,
using Crawmer's techniques, to make the difference for dogs who
arrive at the shelter with behavior problems. "These dogs can be
turned around, *before* they are adopted," says Marchand, "so
maybe they won't come back."

Marchand is the first shelter president with dog expertise. Born in Waterford, New York, just north of Troy, she grew up next door to her grandparents' dairy farm. "They had cows, turkeys, some pigs and horses, and a couple of dogs. We used to watch them pluck the chickens," she recalls. (Today, she's a vegetarian.) As a child, Charlene collected stray dogs and cats, but they were only allowed as far as the front porch. Nevertheless, her obsession with animals came later. Her first passion was the Catholic church.

"My parents were very religious, and I went to Catholic schools my whole life," she says. "In my junior year of high school I made the commitment to become a nun, and my parents prepared my dowry. One month after I graduated, I entered the convent in Albany. I was eighteen years old, and my goal was to become a missionary doctor and travel to Africa and India. I felt I had a vocation."

Charlene's first year in the convent was both "thrilling" and "difficult." She describes this period in her life as a time when she became closer to God but depressed about her isolation in the nunnery. Finally, she realized that she needed to leave; her lifework was outside the confines of the convent. Charlene moved back home and began working in social services. Then one night her life changed. "I met Michael Wilson in a bar," says Charlene, as she tosses her long blond hair and her blue eyes light up. "I moved in with him two weeks later. And you can imagine how my parents felt. Nice girls don't move in with their boyfriends!"

Three years later they were married, and her parents learned to love Michael, too. He's the one who had always wanted a German shepherd. Charlene says, "I just wanted a dog—I didn't care what kind as long as it had four legs." Their first one, Urram (an Indian word which means "right way"), gave birth to two puppies who grew up and became champion service dogs in police canine units. Charlene is not the kind of woman who does anything halfheartedly. Within several years she was breeding, training, and rescuing shepherds, along with volunteering at the Humane Society. She had become president of her regional German Shepherd club. Today she has five shepherds and often comments that "Heaven for me will be one continuous dog show."

I walk through the shelter kennel with Charlene one day, and she takes a quick look at Hunter, a German shorthaired pointer sitting in a cage, and says, "That dog is aggressive. He shouldn't be put up for adoption."

"How can you tell?" I ask her. Hunter seems like a fine fellow to me.

"By the look in his eyes," she says. "I can't explain it."

The following day, Hunter takes an unprovoked bite out of a kennel worker's ankle.

I have never met anyone who can size up a dog as quickly as Charlene. She seems to work partly on instinct and body language, just like them. There's a terrier mix named Honey in the kennel whom I really like; Marchand says the dog is nuts. Honey is adopted and returned within days for neurotic behavior. Once back, she immediately goes cage-crazy, hysterically twirling in her kennel and backing up when people approach her. I ask Camille Praga, who is caring for her, what she thinks of Honey. "The dog is completely mad," she responds, rolling her eyes. "I have trouble just getting her in and out of the kennel." Marchand was absolutely right.

Charlene is concerned about the staff's ability to distinguish aggressive dogs from borderline ones. Her speciality is correcting aggressive behavior, and she wants to teach the kennel workers to do more temperament testing. This is the way the professionals— trainers, breeders, rescuers, veterinarians—weed out dangerous dogs. She decides to demonstrate her technique on a dog named Axle, who came from a family where there was acknowledged do- mestic violence. The dog was starving on arrival and had a history of biting. But the staff had no reason to put any credence in the surrenderer's story; they presumed that Axle is not aggressive but was badly beaten and neglected. They want to save the dog, an ap- pealing longhaired collie mix with big brown eyes, who is terrified of people. Axle has been in the shelter for three days. From Laura- Ann's perspective, he's a prime candidate for euthanasia if she needs kennel space.

Camille brings out the dog as the shelter staff gathers in the parking lot to watch the demonstration. Axle, who is unkempt, looks nervous. Camille holds the leash while Marchand begins. The dog is working with her reluctantly. "Dogs have very sensitive feet," says Marchand. "If you can pinch a dog's toe, that's the mo- ment they will show a bite response if they have it in them." Mar- chand grabs the dog's toe and gives it a pinch. The dog responds with a growl. Camille is still holding the leash but backing away. Kate, my daughter, jumps up onto the roof of a car to get as far from the action as possible. But Marchand is not the least bit put off. She goes for another toe, and Axle growls again, showing a set of large, sharp teeth.

Undeterred, the fearless trainer gives the dog one last pinch, pushing him over the edge. Axle explodes in a blur of motion, lunges for her forearm, ripping through her skin with his teeth. After the initial attack, the dog doesn't back off, but digs in, shredding her arm. Amazingly, Marchand remains cool and instructs Camille how to pull the dog off her body.

The staffers are horrified, rush to Charlene's side. The wound looks like it was made with a chain saw, but it is she who calms everyone down. "Bites go with the territory," she says matter-of-factly, wrapping her bleeding arm in a bandage. "From now on we have to muzzle the dogs when we do this."

Marchand goes to the hospital for stitches, and Axle is returned to his cage. He will not be going home again. But that evening, Charlene comes to the shelter after everyone has gone and feeds Axle some chunks of raw beef. It's his last supper. "I needed to make peace with him," she tells me later, with moist eyes. This woman loves dogs.

Indisputable biters, however, are not handed out to the public. They are terminated. "Fear-biters" present a different set of challenges because they are unpredictable and more difficult to identify. Unlike overtly aggressive dogs, who usually let people know their sentiments right away, fear biters are generally friendly and docile until something, or someone, sets them off. Fear-biters often attach themselves to one person; others are not safe around them unless they receive some serious training. The idea is to induce the behavior that needs to be corrected and correct it on the spot. In the right hands, these dogs are fine.

Lori Beckers is probably the best person at Columbia-Greene when it comes to assessing a fear-biter. She has no interest in adopting them out and then watching people bring them right back. Beckers and Andrea Walker often have diametrically opposed views on the potential, or adoptability, of a dog.

"Princess is a fear-biter," Lori announces right away when the dog first comes in. "I wouldn't trust that dog in my house for a second." Her comments, which can be fatal for any shelter animal, are never made lightly. The dog, a cocker mix, is not responding to her, and she is trying to coax her out of her shell. Princess was surrendered for being "nippy," but many dogs surrendered for this reason turn out to be just fine when placed in homes with no children. "Most of them warm up to me, but not this little one," Lori says. But Princess has her charms. Andrea wants to move her into the main kennel where the public can see her. She feels strongly about the dog. It is difficult for Laura-Ann to refuse any dog a chance when he or she has an advocate. The director frequently manages to say no, but this time, she agrees to put Princess up for adoption.

Moving from the boarding building, where dogs spend their first days, to the main building can be stressful. Princess loses ground in the transition; she retreats to the back of her cage. Andrea works harder, with some success, to reacclimate the dog. She brings her into the front office after a few days. "Look at her," she tells me. "Look at how far this dog has come." Princess is bopping around, sniffing everyone fearlessly. She's still a little hand-shy, but the dog seems much more trusting around people. Some days the little dog is fine. Some days she's spooked.

But after a few weeks in the shelter, Princess is so anxious that she begins to chew at her own skin, which is not uncommon. Dogs, like people, can develop nervous tics, and they have stress responses to being caged. Soon, Princess has a hot spot—a nasty open sore on her side—which does not make her more appealing to the public. Without Andrea, she probably would have been euthanized weeks earlier. Now she needs medical attention.

On the day of her vet appointment, Andrea is too busy to take her. Lori is making the run. I take Princess from her kennel easily; the dog likes me. But when she sees that I am going to put her in a car, she goes flat on her belly and gives me an awful look. I try to win the dog's confidence back, but her scowls escalate into growls. After Axle, there's no way I'm going to push this dog. "You city people," says Lori facetiously, as she takes the leash from my hand. Now the dog is getting really upset.

"Wait, let me get Andrea," I suggest, running off to find her. But "Becker the Wrecker" is not about to ask for help. When I return to the front parking lot, Lori has put Princess in the van, but her arm is ripped open, bleeding. "It's nothing," Lori says cheerfully, hiding her wound. "There's no reason to make a big deal out of this, but you can't put this dog up for adoption." Then she drives off to Dr. Johnson's office.

I go back into the office to tell Laura-Ann that Lori has been bitten. The director is very upset. She immediately grabs the dog's file to see if Princess is up-to-date on her rabies vaccine. The file indicates that she is, but Laura-Ann wants to be sure. She calls the veterinarian's office herself to check that the dog got the shot. Fortunately, the dog was vaccinated; Lori is safe. Next, Laura-Ann puts in a call to Dr. Johnson's office. Princess is not coming back to the shelter, and a sample of her brain tissue will be checked for rabies. (After all bites, the state requires the animal to be either euthanized and tested for rabies or quarantined.) After completing these tasks in a businesslike fashion, the director turns to me and says, "Do you still want to see a puppy mill?"

"I think so," I respond.

"We've been enlisted, along with eight other shelters, to participate in a raid. The Mohawk and Hudson River Humane Society has finally got enough evidence against this breeder," Laura-Ann tells me. "I just got a call from Sue McDonough. She thinks a judge is about to issue a warrant." McDonough is a state trooper and an expert in animal cruelty. She is also the president of the New York State Humane Society. "They need help taking the dogs out, and I've volunteered to house some of them here," she adds.

"When will it happen?" I ask.

"Who knows?" she says. "Could be next week. Could be a year from now. Depends on how the judge feels about dogs." The director laughs and moves on to her next phone call.

TWO MONTHS AFTER Lee and I visited April King's home, her boyfriend walks into the shelter when I am at the counter. The man is upset about something, and he lights up a cigarette, which is not allowed inside the building. (The No Smoking sign argues for the protection of the animals, not the employees.) "Where's April?" I ask him. He points to the car, where April is sitting in the front seat with her black-and-white pup in her arms.

"We just can't do it," the boyfriend tells me. "We just can't train her. She messes on the floor, won't walk on the leash. It's too much work." He's exasperated and tired. I can see that bringing the dog in was a big decision for them both. I thank him for coming to the shelter and quickly give him the appropriate form to fill out before April changes her mind. As he signs the document, he says, "We're thinking of getting a cat because they're much less work." Given the fate of April's last cat, this is not a brilliant idea. "Have you ever been bitten by a cat?" I ask him as I complete the paperwork. He doesn't answer.

As soon as he signs the animal surrender form, the dog is shelter property. I'm anxious to go outside and see both April and the dog. When I appear, leash in hand, April doesn't seem the least bit upset about giving up her pup. "Any problems with her?" I ask April.

"I'm pregnant," she says, with a wide grin on her face. "It's too much work to have a dog now."

I'm speechless. I force myself to wish her good luck, and I take the puppy from her arms.

I am wondering if the shelter should feel an obligation to report this pregnancy to a child-welfare agency. The links between animal and child abuse are obvious. The American Humane Association has had both child and animal protection divisions since its inception in the late 1800s. This organization runs seminars to train humane officers to recognize signs of abuse and report children who are in danger. Some states, in an attempt to amplify the relationship between animal and child abuse, have made it mandatory for humane officers to report suspected abusers, which is a fitting direction for the animal welfare movement to take.

In less than a year, social services will take April King's baby from her arms for the same reasons that the Humane Society took away her dogs.

Rouge (a.k.a. Shotgun), rescued
from the Ponderosa Fun Park

FIVE

"The Eyes Can't Trespass"

Barbara Dohrman has received two complaints on a thin horse in the village of Leeds, just outside of Catskill. The horse is visible from the road. "Someone has got to go out and check that mare so I can stop worrying about her," Dohrman says to Laura-Ann. The investigators are all part-time due to financial constraints, and Dohrman is continually frustrated because there is no one to send out. She advises people in emergencies to call the police, but the police are not well versed in the laws that protect animals. A handful of local officers who like animals respond; most have more important matters to worry about.

Complaints about animals come in continually, but only a small percentage turn out to be situations where the shelter can or should intervene. Humane officers have a tough job. Every case requires a tremendous amount of work, and rarely do they pan out. Most reports turn out to be exaggerated or based on misinformation. Frequently the animals are not in great shape but not sick enough for officers to seize them. The courts have little interest in any animal abuse cases, let alone a borderline one. It takes forever to get any legal action.

Lee DeLisle is extremely realistic about his limitations. The Humane Society receives many complaints on horses, but he is careful not to seize more large animals than the shelter can comfortably house; the barn is small. Two weeks after the initial report on Leeds, DeLisle and I are on our way to find that horse.

Leeds is in Greene County. We drive across the Rip Van Winkle Bridge, a little south of Hudson, heading toward the Catskill Mountains. Although DeLisle frequently goes out on complaints involving all kinds of animals, he is unabashedly partial to horses. Earning his living as a farrier, he spends much of his time underneath them, checking their feet and forging shoes that perfectly fit the idiosyncratic shape of each hoof. DeLisle is a craftsman who carefully tracks every new horseshoeing method and tool, attending professional conferences and workshops all over the country. In America, professional farriers are members of the American Farriers Association, a self-regulated organization that is free of government restraints but religious in its zeal to monitor and perfect the practice. In England, where some of the most skillful farriers in the world can be found, it is illegal for people to shoe their own horses; farriers are licensed along with veterinarians. "Here anyone can shoe a horse," says DeLisle. The professionals have to clean up the results.

Lee is a highly trained investigator, having gone through courses at the Law Enforcement Training Institute (one of the most prestigious schools for investigators worldwide), which makes him unique in this field. He is also the recipient of the Toni Hanna Memorial Award, given annually by the New York State Humane Association for excellence in the field. As a local farrier, he knows most of the horses in the area, and if he doesn't know them, chances are one of his buddies will. Farriers and their clients, quite naturally, gossip about horse people, often tipping Lee off to situations where there are animals in need. One of the two complaints about the horse in Leeds came from a client.

Leeds is about five minutes west of the bridge. It's not especially prosperous, but a typical village with country roads lined by small houses that are separated by ample yards. We pull into the driveway of a two-story clapboard house that looks neglected, ravaged by weather and hard times. A fat pony is standing in a paddock adjacent to the house with a very thin mare. She's a tall, bony chestnut with a black mane; her withers pop up out of her back and slope down like a steep hill. The pony, a chocolate Shetland with a blond mane, looks like she's been getting the lion's share of hay.

Without the horses, the house would look almost abandoned. Every window on the first floor is obscured by shades or some sort of opaque material, making it difficult to see in. There's so much junk on the porch we have to negotiate a trail to the front door, which we do before Lee starts banging on it, shouting, "Anyone home?" A couple of dogs begin to bark. A faint chorus of birds is also audible from the porch. It's difficult to tell how many birds and dogs are inside. We notice a fan in a side window blowing air into the first floor of the house, and a lamp turned on inside. "Someone's home," says Lee.

A solitary black rabbit sits in a cage by the front steps. There's a tired-looking strand of alfalfa in the cage and a bottle of water that is half full. Lee keeps banging on the door, but only the dogs respond, barking like crazy. Some people might consider the dogs a deterrent. Not Lee. He keeps on banging, and the dogs keep on barking, and the birds keep on singing. When he stops briefly, the dogs stop, too. After the fourth round of this, we walk to the paddock through a yard that is covered with debris. Oddly enough, there's a garden area carefully delineated with rocks and a few plantings of the usual annuals, mostly petunias, traces of a happier time when the place wasn't so shabby. A Chevy truck with a large bag of horse feed in the back is parked in the driveway; a still legible Clinton/Gore sticker is stuck to the rear bumper.

"So, I guess no one's home," I say.

"Oh, someone's home, all right," he responds. "Let's look at the horse." He walks over to the moving skeleton. When the light hits her profile, it throws her rib cage into relief. As Lee approaches the animals, they retreat to an open shed. "They need to get away from the flies," he says. "Neither of them have any protection. I hate that."

The investigator explains that it would be trespassing if we entered the paddock to see the horse, adding, "If it were an emergency, it would be different." We return to the house, walking around to the rear in search of a back door. On the way, we meet a filthy yellow dog, a Lab mix with an orange nose, chained to a post in the hot sun. No water, food, or shelter in sight.

I leave Lee banging on the back door and walk up to the dog.

She stops barking when I approach, lies down on her back, and wags her tail. She's submissive. When I get close enough to touch her, I realize that the dog looks as bad as the horse; her ribs are architectural, jutting out of her sides. She walks slowly like an old dog, but her teeth age her at around two or three. Her fur is falling out, and there are open sores, probably from bugs, on both ears. The dog likes having her head rubbed. I call Lee over.

"Look how thin this dog is," I say. He shakes his head and takes out his camera; he photographs her ears and her sides. "We can put her in the car and take her to the shelter right now," I suggest. "Hold on," he says. "Not so fast." Lee doesn't grab animals on the spot unless they are in real danger.

I assume we are going to walk into the yard behind the house to check out some other animals we can hear in the back, but Lee doesn't want to do anything else without a search warrant. "We have a complaint about the horse, which is in public view from the road," he explains. "By law, we have the right to knock on the front door and get permission to see the animals. If no one answers the door, we have the right to walk around the house to see if there's a back entrance. As we walk around the house, we can check any animals we incidentally come upon who might be suffering. This is why we could check out the dog." The man dots his i's and crosses his t's. "But we cannot simply walk through her grounds looking for other animals without a search warrant," he says again. "If she charges us with trespassing, it could jeopardize our ability to take out any animals."

"I'm worried about the dog."

"Based on the condition of the horse and the dog, I'll have more than ample probable cause for a warrant. We're not going to take the dog now, but we'll be back," he assures me. "Don't worry."

"I don't think anybody should have the right to keep an animal the way this woman is keeping her dog," I reply. "If we wait, she might come home, realize the animal cops have been to her house, and hide the dog, along with any other animals she might have who are in bad shape."

Lee gives me a look which makes me realize that I'm way out of line. I'm having a PETA moment.

"I want you to understand why I'm not going to take this dog," Lee says in a serious tone. "I'm not an animal rights activist. I'm an animal welfare investigator. You and I see this dog from two entirely different points of view. You see a suffering dog who needs emergency care. I see a cruelty case that I don't want to lose."

Then he tells me a story about two dogs in a cage up on a nearby mountain in the Catskills. "The house was owned by New Yorkers who were getting divorced and selling the place, and the dogs were left there all week alone. Sometimes the man or the woman came on weekends; sometimes no one showed up at all. I watched the place, day and night, for a week in February. The weather was going to drop below zero, and no one was taking care of the dogs. I knew it could take a few days to locate the owners and obtain a search warrant, and by that time the dogs would be dead. So I went in and took the dogs and brought them to the shelter. The dogs were adopted in a week, and the people never even filed a missing report on their animals.

"Now what if we take this dog today and we bring her to a vet, which we must do by law, and the vet says, 'Well, she's undernourished, has worms, and her ears need some ointment.' Is the dog in immediate danger of death?" It's a rhetorical question. "Meanwhile, this dog's owner goes out and gets herself a hand-wringing liberal lawyer to take her case, and he convinces the jury that her civil rights were violated when we trespassed onto her property and took her dog," he continues. "So all the charges are dropped because of a sloppy seizure. And then she slaps the Humane Society with a lawsuit for ruining her reputation in the community."

Lee reminds me that at this point we don't even know the woman's name. "We have to be able to convince a jury that we acted as reasonable people. Are you a reasonable person?" he asks me.

"On occasion," I answer him.

"Come on," says the pet detective congenially. "There's more work to do." On the other side of the horse pen is a run-down motel called the Mountain Rest Stop that seems to be closed. It's a place where time stopped at least a decade ago. When Lee knocks on the door of the big house, a voice shouts, "Come on in."

An elderly man and woman are sitting at a kitchen table eating salami sandwiches and reading newspapers as if they've been doing this together forever. As motel proprietors, they are relaxed enough to welcome strangers right into their kitchen. Lee hands them his card and explains why we are standing here watching them eat lunch. The kitchen, vintage fifties linoleum and appliances, is spotless.

Both the innkeeper and his wife are thrilled when they understand the purpose of our visit. These folks know their neighbor's name. "Lucy Hall," the man says right away. "Been in court with her twice trying to get her evicted. But she's got friends in high places." He says Hall lives there with her fourteen-year-old son. "She put us out of business," he adds. "Couldn't ask people to stay here and smell the stench, all that chicken shit," his wife chimes in.

"Excuse my language," she adds. She points out her window at a tall fence that separates their properties. "What do you think that fence is for?" she says. "Haven't had a decent night of sleep in years because of those damn roosters."

"There are no zoning ordinances in this town," the old man explains. "She can do whatever she wants over there." He continues to complain but with little enthusiasm. It's clear that they have given up the battle. "She doesn't keep the place up, but she's real smart," the man warns us. "If the car is in the driveway, she's definitely there," the woman says, swallowing the food in her mouth. "I know she's home."

We return to Hall's house. Lee tapes a warning ticket on her front door which gives Hall twenty-four hours to contact the Humane Society. Before he leaves, some instinct makes him pound on the door one last time. Within seconds it opens, and a chubby weimaraner comes flying out and disappears into the backyard. Then a sleepy, disheveled boy appears, rubbing his eyes.

"Is your mother home?" asks Lee.

"Naw," says the kid. He's not wearing a shirt, and his pants are so loose they look like they might slip off any second. I can't believe he's slept through all the barking and commotion, but then again, he's a teenager.

"Where's your mother?" Lee asks brusquely.

"What do *you* want with her?" he shoots back at the investigator.

"When is she coming home?" Lee asks again.

"Who wants to know?"

Lee has no intention of getting into an argument with a fourteen-year-old boy. He hands him his card and briefly explains the nature of the ticket; he instructs him to have his mother get in touch with the Humane Society immediately to talk about her animals. As he turns around to leave, the boy slams the front door.

Lee and I get into the car, and he starts to relax a little. "This case is going to be a big pain before it's over," he says. I'm not quite sure what he means. "You'll see. It's likely that this woman has managed to survive on the edge for years. She probably has bill collectors after her, owes the government taxes, and now the Humane Society is coming in to hassle her about the care of her animals," he continues sympathetically. "We don't really know much about her, what she does for a living, or how the town feels about her. You can't go by neighbors. Half the cases I go out on are just territorial disputes, where one side wants to use the shelter against the other."

We have just spent almost two hours peeking into Lucy Hall's life, learning very little. There's no way to tell why her horse is so thin, or if there are a hundred more neglected animals hidden in her backyard. It could go either way. Hall could be a collector or simply a person struggling to hold on to her animals. "Whatever happens, I'm going to find out what's she's feeding that mare," he assures me. I have no doubt he will.

Before returning to the shelter, Lee has one more case in Greene County. We head up to East Jewett, a sparsely populated mountain town in the Catskills. The drive is spectacular, through a rolling landscape dotted with funky motels, log cabins, and hidden chalets. Greene County is more lush and rural than Columbia County.

We are on our way to the Rough Riders Ranch, a trail-riding operation up in the mountains and largely out of sight. This is one of those cases that DeLisle has been working on for months. Back in October 1996, Lee arrested a man named Joe D'Acunto, the Rough Rider himself, and seized two of his horses. I saw the horses as he unloaded them into the barn at the shelter; they were starving and coughing, suffering from severe upper respiratory problems. The case, almost one year later, is still pending in the courts. It is likely that it will never go to trial because there aren't enough people in Jewett to convene a proper jury. This is precisely why some people choose to live up in the mountains.

Meanwhile, despite the Humane Society's efforts, Mr. D'Acunto decided to add a petting zoo to the ranch. But he failed to get the necessary permits for his new sideshow. Under pressure from the Jewett town planning board, he was encouraged to get his paperwork in order; D'Acunto put in an application for the required permit. To no one's surprise, the shelter received a complaint from one of the first visitors to the zoo. The animals, the woman claimed, were living in squalor. Before the investigator had a chance to go up to Jewett and see the farm animals for himself, he received another call from a Jewett town councilman, requesting information on D'Acunto's October arrest. The board felt the case might have some bearing on whether they should grant D'Acunto a permit for the zoo.

Lee agreed to testify at the next planning-board meeting, which is nine days away. Today he wants to get a peek at D'Acunto's animals, if possible, from a public road that runs by the ranch.

The main attraction at the Rough Riders Ranch is Joe himself, who, Lee has been told, dresses up in a nineteenth-century cavalry outfit (blue uniform, high black boots, saber in hand) and leads tourists through the mountains as if he were leading the cavalry into battle. According to his own promotional material, Sergeant Joe D., as he calls himself, was a member of the ceremonial horse platoon of the First Cavalry Division, Fort Hood, Texas.

D'Acunto's legal hassles apparently haven't curtailed his ambitions or plans to expand. He has acquired new horses and farm animals to attract business and produced myriad flyers advertising "overnight riding adventures" and "private catered parties for all occasions."

When we arrive, Lee parks on the side of the road and takes binoculars and a camera out of his bag. He looks at me with a smile on his face and says, "We're just going to take a country walk down a public road. The eyes can't trespass," he adds.

"Is Joe going to be here?" I suddenly want to know.

"Don't know," says Lee, as he puts on a blue jacket which says HUMANE LAW ENFORCEMENT AGENT in large white letters on the back. "Lock up the car, and let's go," he says in a cheery voice. We start down the road.

Right off, we see a mare just a few feet from the road in a narrow pen, about the size of an average living room, pitched on an incline. The horse has to do a kind of balancing act to stay upright, but at least she has a pile of hay and a tub of water. She's friendly (or maybe hungry) and comes right over to greet us. I stroke her nose as Lee checks her out. "She's thin, borderline," he says right away, not pleased. We can see her ribs and not much flesh on top of them. I'm thinking, Well, she looks better than Lucy Hall's horse, which is no recommendation. I point out some goop dripping from one of the mare's eyes. "That's just from the flies," he says.

It's hard to know why the horse is so thin. Lee would have to observe her over a period of time to see if she is being fed regularly.

He explains that working horses need some grain added to their diets, especially during the summer, but some people only feed them hay. Others don't believe in feeding their horses any hay at all and only let them graze. But there's nothing to graze on here but rocks and dirt. There are certainly no laws governing what people should feed horses, but there are legal standards of acceptable body weights. Lee wants to come back and "body score" all D'Acunto's horses on a system developed to examine the body fat of large animals. This horse, Lee says, "should weigh about 1,000 pounds, but she looks like she weighs about 825." Right now, however, Lee can't get near any of the horses because doing so would require trespassing on D'Acunto's land.

We can hear more horses just out of sight around a curve down the road, but there's a car coming slowly toward us. "Here we go," says Lee. It's the Rough Rider, of course, bouncing along in his Jeep Cherokee.

Sergeant Joe D. slams on the brakes, and Lee goes over to speak with him through the window opposite the driver's side. I don't move, sort of pretending to be more interested in the horse. I can't hear what they're saying, but I can see Joe through the windshield becoming more and more agitated. Lee is not raising his voice, but he's arguing and showing visible signs of frustration. Then he reaches down into his pocket and starts fishing around for something. For a second, I think he's going to pull out a gun, but instead he produces a small tape recorder, which he turns on. Joe just keeps on talking and gesticulating. "Come on over here," Lee abruptly calls out to me. "I want a witness for this conversation."

I walk over and stand near Lee, partly for my own protection. Joe is still sitting in his car, and although he hardly looks dangerous,

I'm hoping he's not going to get out. He's got a headful of curly brown hair and a pudgy face. He's ranting at Lee: "You've got a personal vendetta against me! There's nothing wrong with my horses—look at her, she's got plenty of hay, she's fenced in. I have another round bale coming in today."

"The horse is borderline, Joe," Lee tells him sternly.

"Look, if you were a civil person, I'd talk to you," D'Acunto responds snottily. "I'd even barbecue with you. But you come here, you break into my trailer and steal my horses."

Lee interrupts him, starting to show his anger. "Joe, I arrested you when I was here last. But let's stick to the present. I don't like the way that mare looks, and you better do something about it because, I assure you, I'll be coming back here."

"There's nothing wrong with her—she's got water and hay. That's just shit," he says, continuing a litany of abuse.

"Would you like to give me permission to see all your horses right now?" asks the investigator.

"No way," Joe says. "This is a private road, and you're trespassing."

"I'm under the impression that this is a public road, but I'll leave right away if it's private. I wouldn't want to violate your rights, Joe. But I'll see you on August 7 at the planning board meeting," Lee adds, giving him a big grin.

"If you were only a nicer person—," continues Joe, still shouting.

"I don't want to be your friend, Joe. I just want to make sure your animals are properly cared for. Why don't you just give me permission to see them right now. Wouldn't that be the easiest thing to do?"

"Get off my property!"

"Let's go," Lee says to me. "This isn't going anywhere." And we start walking back up the road. "I *will* find out whether or not this is a public road," Lee calls to Joe over his shoulder. The Cherokee is moving slowly, following us up the road.

"Do you think he's going to try and run us over?" I whisper to Lee.

"He's a wimp," he responds. "Don't worry about a thing." I find myself walking quickly to the car, unlocking it, and leaping in. As Lee turns on the engine, Joe comes running up to his window carrying a dirty wooden sign that he seems to have unearthed from the side of the road. "You see this?" he shouts, holding it about a foot from Lee's face. "Read it!" It's difficult to read, but the old sign once indicated PRIVATE ROAD.

As we drive into Jewett to find the town clerk and check the legal status of Woodlands Road, Lee tells me the story of his first encounter with Mr. D'Acunto. After receiving several complaints about a group of horses boarded on Boy Scout campgrounds, which is where Joe used to keep his horses, Lee went out to investigate. It was October, and he wanted to make sure the horses were being taken care of before the weather changed.

"I watched the horses for forty-eight hours, visiting them day and night, taking photographs. Every time I came to see them," Lee recalls, "they were so thirsty they rushed up to me, hoping I was going to water them." But the investigator couldn't do that. Instead, he carefully documented their misery, hoping to obtain a warrant that would enable him to investigate more thoroughly. He gave D'Acunto a warning and thirty days to improve the condition of the horses. But their condition didn't improve.

"The morning I went to arrest him, it was pouring rain," Lee remembers. "I had a friend with me driving a horse trailer, in case I needed to take any horses, but all I was planning to do was give Joe an appearance ticket to get him into court on neglect charges, and leave. I knocked on his trailer door, and when he came out, I asked him if we could step inside for a minute to get out of the rain. He said, 'No.' So I'm giving him his Miranda rights in this downpour, getting soaked to the bone, when this slime turned and ran into his trailer to hide from me. Then he sneaked out a back window, and I saw him running down the road!" Lee chased him for a quarter of a mile and caught him.

"When I finally had him, he gave me a hard time," he continues. "I had to pin him against the side of my truck and cuff him. He dented my truck! Joe claims I assaulted him." Lee chuckles. D'Acunto did not press any charges against him, but DeLisle added two counts of resisting arrest to the eight charges of animal cruelty. He ended up taking Joe down to police headquarters, hauling the two sickest horses in a trailer behind him. Countess and Brutus arrived at the shelter covered in mud, starving, and breathing with difficulty.

The horses are currently in foster care under the shelter's jurisdiction, waiting for the outcome of the case. "You wouldn't recognize them now," Lee tells me. "They're both doing so beautifully. One of them can never be ridden again as a result of respiratory problems, but both are going to be fine." Watching the horses he rescues fill out and begin to thrive is Lee's reward. "I hope these two will never have to move anywhere again. Their foster owners want to keep them permanently."

When Lee and I find the East Jewett town clerk in the municipal building, she determines that Woodlands Road is indeed not a public, town-maintained road. "But just because the town isn't responsible for maintaining a road doesn't necessarily mean that the public can't walk on it," she tells us, grinning. The next step is the town's planning-board meeting. DeLisle alerts the clerk that he will be present. "So will Mr. D'Acunto," she tells us. "And the fur is going to fly!"

By the time we pull into the Athens shelter, about a half hour from Jewett, there's a message for Lee to call Lucy Hall. Lee reaches her right away, and I hear him screaming into the phone, "Am I going to have to shout louder than you to be heard, Mrs. Hall?" Then he says calmly into the phone, "I did not threaten your son, Mrs. Hall. I don't go around threatening teenagers, but had *you* been there, I might have arrested you," he adds. With this comment, the woman goes ballistic.

They argue intensely about the weight on the horse, what point old horses should be put down, and the condition of the dog in her backyard. Finally Lee says, "If you want me to come back with a search warrant and arrest you, I will. If you want to give me permission to come back and check your horse and the dog, then I won't have to arrest you. It's your choice, Mrs. Hall."

After a few more minutes, Hall calms down and agrees to let Lee come back to examine the horse, the dog, and any other animals he wants to see. She claims the horse is just old, a "hard-keeper," going downhill. "I don't think so," Lee insists. "But if I'm wrong, that's fine. At least we'll know."

One week later, Lee and I are back at Lucy Hall's house with

Sue Pesano, the new animal-care supervisor at the shelter; Andrea Walker has gone back to school full-time. Pesano is about forty-five and has been assisting veterinarians for over ten years. She grew up in Columbia County, and she knows the mentality of the community—what they did and did not learn in school, what they think of their animals, and what they drink at night. For years, she was the bartender, among other things, at the Carolina House, a local barbecue restaurant in Kinderhook. She's also a dog person, and Lee wants her to check out Hall's dog.

Hall is standing in her driveway talking on a cell phone; there are two men by her side. She looks fortyish and solid, like she's been through it all. Her dark hair is pulled back out of her face and held in a no-nonsense clip. The guys, I assume, are her moral support, but she looks tougher than either one of them. She telegraphs her attitude toward us instantly: she's in a rage.

Lee introduces Sue and myself to Hall and turns on a tape recorder as he is speaking. He is explaining that it is always better to have an official record in case any problems arise, but Hall interrupts him. "Hold on," she snaps when her cell phone rings.

"Dr. Alamo's answering service," she says. "Can I help you? No, the doctor's unavailable. Do you want me to beep him? Right." She hangs up.

"I run an answering service," she informs us. "So bear with me." The phone rings again.

"Dr. Alamo's answering service." She has tiny slips of paper in her hand and a pen; she's trying to give out information, take messages, and watch us, all at the same time.

DeLisle, Pesano, and I walk into the paddock. Lee opens the horse's mouth right away, checking to see if her teeth are properly floated. (He is also a trained equine dentist.) If the horse's teeth weren't cared for, this might prevent her from chewing her food and properly digesting it. "The teeth are fine," Lee concludes.

"I told you so," says Hall. "There's nothing wrong with this horse." The phone rings.

"Carting and Moving," she answers. "Hi. Yes." She hangs up. The phone rings again. "Dr. Lowenstein's office. Can I help you? That's right. Do you need the number? Bye." She hangs up.

Lee is examining the horse's body, lifting up her tail, looking in her ears, up her nostrils. He pinches some skin and pulls it away from her body. "She's badly dehydrated," he tells Hall.

"When you came here last week, you found food, clean water, and fresh bedding, didn't you?" says Hall in an argumentative manner.

"Yes, I did," says Lee. "And the horse was in extremely poor condition and remains so."

"I can run through a list of everything I've done to keep weight on her," she offers. The list is long. "She's old," Hall continues. "She's just old. She was already an old unwanted horse when I took her in."

"Can we look at the dog now?" asks Lee.

We walk toward the back of the house. Hall is well into a monologue on how much she loves her animals. "No one takes better care of their animals. I do everything for them," she tells us repeatedly.

The dog actually looks a little better than the last time we were here. She's more lively. There's a homemade doghouse off in a corner of the yard that we could not see from where we were standing. I thought it was just a junk pile, but it's a box filled with hay, which is probably where the bugs are coming from that are eating the dog's ears. Lucy rubs the dog's belly and sprays her ears with some kind of medicine. "She's on heartworm, she's spayed, and her name is Cassie."

"What do you think, Sue?" Lee asks. "How does the dog look to you?

"I've seen worse," says Sue honestly. "The dog is energetic." She checks the dog's ears and says, "She's got bad mites."

"No, she doesn't," retorts Hall. "That's just dirt. She rubs herself in the dirt all the time." Hall has an answer for everything. "I spray her ears every day," she insists. Sue backs off.

Lee and Hall move toward an area filled with about a dozen rabbit pens, and I have a minute alone with Sue. "You really think the dog's OK?" I ask.

"It's not the way you or I would care for a dog, but she's just a skinny dirty outside dog with bad ears." I'm not convinced, but she's the expert.

Pesano walks over to get the spray bottle that Hall has used on the dog's ears. She sprays some on her arm and gives it a sniff.

"Water!" she says. "It's just water!" For some reason we both find this very funny.

"Look at that goat," I tell Sue, pointing to an old fat goat on a cable wire under some trees. "The goat looks pregnant."

"There's only one goat," Sue points out. "Who do you think got her, one of the roosters?"

Sue and I go to check out the rabbits, walking through an area where Hall has ducks, roosters, and hens. The wire rabbit hutches are clean and orderly; every animal has a bowl of food and water, although no bedding. "They don't need any," Hall tells me when I inquire. I'm not going to argue with her.

"Dr. Alamo's service. Right. Bye."

The rabbit area is littered with animal hair and junked cages. "I don't take such good care of my place, but I take care of my animals," she says. "Lucy drove to New York City once to pick up a cat that was being mistreated," one of the guys tells us. Adds Hall, "I didn't just clean this place up for you people."

There are no animal sounds coming from the house today, which seems strange. Hall doesn't invite us into her home to meet her birds, if there are any.

Lee is getting ready to leave, and I can see him trying to figure out the best way to conclude the inspection. The sun is beating down on us; it's one of those sweaty, hot days. I find myself feeling a little badly for Lucy Hall. She does seem to love her animals, despite the fact that the farm is out of control. This whole scene, animals and people, is spiraling downhill, and she is trying to keep it from crashing. She's broke, struggling to launch her own business, a single mother, and overwhelmed by the needs of her animals.

Finally Lee says, "I'll give you till next Tuesday. Either you have a vet report about that horse on my desk, or I'll be back with a search warrant and a veterinarian. If there's anything wrong with the horse, we'll take her with us. If she's well, then we can all be thankful."

"Where do you think you're going to get a search warrant?"

"That won't be difficult to obtain, I assure you."

"Well, if it's from the local Catskill judge, I don't think so. Who do you think answers calls for the judge?"

"Guess I won't be leaving any messages for the judge," Lee quips, as we drive back to the shelter.

The following week, Hall herself delivers the doctor's report to the shelter. She is still in a rage. The horse has no worms or other illnesses, confirming her diagnosis. The mare is just old, going downhill, and simply not long for this world. Lee is satisfied with the report, although disappointed the vet failed to prescribe a special diet. "But this is all the Humane Society can do," he says. "It was our responsibility to make sure that horse wasn't sick, and we did." The case is closed. DeLisle can add Lucy Hall to his enemies list.

THERE ARE ABOUT a dozen people milling around the town hall parking lot on Thursday evening, August 7. Laura-Ann, Lee, and I get there before Mr. D'Acunto. By the time Michael Bolz, chairman of the planning board, shows up and unlocks the building about thirty more people have arrived. The crowd is unusually large for a planning-board meeting in East Jewett, so the event is moved to a bigger room upstairs. "We're about to see democracy in action," Laura-Ann says to me. I can't tell if people in the room are here to see D'Acunto rise to this occasion or to watch him fall.

The Rough Rider is sitting in the front row, wearing high black boots, riding pants, suspenders, and a wide-brimmed hat, which he removes. The chairman explains that Mr. D'Acunto is applying for a special-use permit to operate a petting zoo at his stable. He does not mention that the zoo is already in operation, in violation of the law. Instead, he clarifies the process: It is likely that the planning board will accept the application tonight and then begin an investigation into D'Acunto's situation; a date will be set for a public hearing. Then, the board will either deny or approve the application.

The spectators in the room, including those of us with the Humane Society, are confused. We were under the impression that tonight's event *was* the public hearing. This is only round one.

Flipping through the application, one board member immediately points out that D'Acunto's property is less than one acre. There's a three-acre zoning law in East Jewett; the Rough Rider Ranch, let alone a petting zoo, needs a special variance. D'Acunto's application also states his intention to build a barn, for which he would need an additional variance. There's a bureaucratic swamp to wade through in front of D'Acunto.

"I would rather be receiving chemotherapy than sitting in this room," Lee whispers to me. It's going to be a long night.

Bolz opens up the meeting to the public. The first woman he calls on looks under thirty and is very pregnant; she already has three children under six who are sitting right next to her. "We bought our property fourteen years ago for its serenity and privacy," she begins in a shaky voice, having prepared a speech. "Joe can handle his horses fine, but the paying strangers he parades through are completely reckless. They get thrown, and the horses are loose trampling through my property. My children aren't safe in their own yard. No horseback-riding business is welcome here."

D'Acunto starts to deny that he ever trespasses on her property, but the chairman quiets him down.

Another woman stands up and starts speaking about her daughter, Barbara Runyon, who couldn't be there tonight. Barbara fell off one of D'Acunto's horses and had two compound fractures. "My daughter is now living on painkillers," she says. "When her lawyer contacted Mr. D'Acunto, he said, 'She was hurt? I don't care. If I have nothing, she gets nothing.'" The woman breaks down and weeps. The man sitting next to her tries to comfort her. When she pulls herself together, she continues. "This accident happened last January. When my daughter got thrown, Joe went over and punched the horse right in the face! I think somebody should do that to him!"

"Want to do it right now?" Joe shouts at her.

The next speaker is this woman's fiancé. His words veritably hum with hatred for D'Acunto. "This man advertises trail rides on less than an acre of land. *Where are the trails?* He's using every-body's property in this area." Then he moves on to another equally contentious topic. "Anyone running a business in this country has to have insurance, liability. We are all liable if somebody falls off a horse on our property. This is why we're all here. Joe's danger-ous—a hazard. You people are the planning board! If you let him get away with this, you're liable, too!" As he sits down, a rumble of agreement resonates through the room. The board members are growing more and more uncomfortable.

"He's got six horses on less than an acre," the man blurts out. "Where are they going to be moved next?"

Joe slings insults right back at each speaker in turn. It's like watching a scene out of *Bonanza*. The mob wants to lynch D'Acunto right now, but the sheriff and his posse are trying to keep the peace until they can arrange for a fair trial. Soon, Ben Cartwright (Lee DeLisle) is going to set them all straight.

Finally, it's his turn. "In September of '96, I had the occasion to respond to a phone-in complaint on horse abuse, and on Septem-ber 17, I had my first contact with Joe D'Acunto and his horses.

Two of the six animals I found, I deemed to be malnourished. One of the two had a festering open sore on the hindquarter. A third one was noticeably lame, and all were in need of veterinary and farrier care. I gave Joe a written warrant that allowed him a thirty-day period to correct the situation. During that initial meeting, the only way Joe responded was to tell me that he had no money to feed himself, how was he going to feed the horses. My concern was not with his personal life; my only concern was for the welfare of the horses on his property."

The room is silent for the first time. Everyone is listening intently to the cruelty officer's narrative.

"On October 17, I returned to the property where the horses are now harbored. When I located Joe at this time, only five of the six horses remained. I advised him that he had not complied with the written warning, and as a result I arrested Joe and charged him with eight misdemeanor counts of cruelty to animals.

"Joe told me last October that he was virtually penniless. Yet he was able to come up with ten thousand dollars as a down payment on this piece of property. Our concern is what conditions will result in wintertime once his business shuts down. Who is going to be paying for and caring for those animals? What we would like to see is that no variance or permission to operate any kind of a business be granted to Mr. D'Acunto, at least until the disposition of these charges in a court of law."

"Can you give us an idea of the amount of land required to comfortably care for one horse?" a board member asks the humane officer.

"The Rutgers University guidelines indicate approximately one full acre per horse. Now, that pertains mainly to a situation where the horse has to subsist on pasture. There are many, many horse owners who keep multiple horses on an acre of land, even less than an acre. They have to, however, be provided with adequate exercise, shelter, and nutrition—good hay and grain all year around—if the pasture situation doesn't exist. From what I saw last year, Mr. D'Acunto was not prepared to take care of one horse, much less six horses."

D'Acunto, for the first time, has no response.

"Are there any requirements of law, beyond those relating to cruelty, as to the facilities required for these animals?" asks another board member.

"The law does not address specifics where shelter is concerned," explains DeLisle. "What it does do is refer to what we call sustenance. In that, the law is very specific referring to 'proper food, water, and sustenance.' Sustenance can mean veterinary care or proper shelter when necessary. Veterinary science knows full well that severe kidney ailments and other respiratory illnesses can result in horses that do not have proper shelter."

"Can you give us an idea of what constitutes abuse?" asks a woman on the board. They are all taking good advantage of their expert witness.

"Four of the charges pertain to the lack of water for a period of almost twenty-four hours. Two of the other charges pertain to malnourishment. Two of the malnourished horses were also suffering from respiratory infection and parasite infestation, both of which required extensive medical care after we seized them and removed them from the property. One horse will never fully recover. She can't be ridden."

"You have these horses in your possession?" asks Bolz.

"They have since been fostered out, but they are under our direct supervision and remain so."

The board members begin addressing D'Acunto. "Are you currently running a stable business?"

"People go riding; they come for lessons," he says, slumping down in his chair. Then he suddenly jumps up, as if he's been bitten by a snake, and points a finger at Lee. "It's *my* property, and since this is not a criminal court, let me add that this man came and assaulted me and took my horses. You're listening to this man, but he's got the same manure coming out of his mouth that comes out of my horse's butt!"

"There's no reason to talk like that!" says Bolz, trying to keep the remainder of the meeting from degenerating into a barroom brawl. We're back in Virginia City with the Cartwrights.

Joe is on his feet, waving papers at the board. "Here's *his* vet report on my horses. They weren't undernourished, they were merely thin. This isn't Russia. If I want to keep my horses in trim condition so they can go up and down the mountains, I can. Read the report! It says, 'no respiratory distress.'" Moving toward Lee, he screams, "I didn't allow him to shoe my horses. There's a conflict of interest here. He has a farrier service, isn't that right?"

"Do you have a farrier business?" asks a member of the board.

"Yes, I do," responds Lee.

"I asked him one time to come and do my horses, and he gave me a staggering—a staggering—price," says Joe dramatically. "I said, 'Forget it, I can't afford that,' and now he's got it in for me."

Lee is not the least bit fazed by this accusation. "He left a message on my machine," he whispers into my ear. "He says he has a bunch of horses that need work. I call him back and quote him the same price I would have quoted anyone, about $240. He says, 'I'll give you $125 and that's it.' So I told him, If you want a bargain, go to Wal-Mart. And I hung up." Lee has to stifle a laugh.

Laura-Ann is stewing over the vet report. She raises her hand. "I was directly involved in the care of the horses when they were at the shelter," she informs the board. "The report that Mr. D'Acunto has given you from the vet that refers to 'no respiratory distress' was written when the horses were examined *after* they had spent a period of time at the shelter!"

"Don't lie, you liar, what are you talkin' about?" Joe hollers at Laura-Ann. The room breaks up into a cacophony of individual conversations.

Then the senior member of the board, much to everyone's surprise, says, "I think we should accept Mr. D'Acunto's application." There's a pause.

"We're not voting yes or no tonight, we're just accepting the application," says another member. "The three-acre zoning problem might be a basis for denying the permit, but you have to accept the application first before you can deny it," he adds, as if the logic of this process makes perfect sense.

"I want to know why he is currently allowed to operate this business at all," responds a third board member. "I just don't understand it," he adds. With this comment, the audience breaks into applause.

"Enforcement isn't our jurisdiction," says Bolz. "It's the town board's."

"Then I think we better meet with the town board and find out why this man is running a riding stable when he's in violation of zoning laws. And now we're talking about giving him a special-use permit!" The audience is thrilled with this outburst, applauding some more.

The senior member quiets the room. Then he says firmly, "I move that we accept Mr. D'Acunto's application." The move is seconded, and a vote is taken quickly. There is only one objection. D'Acunto's application has been accepted so that it can be pushed along in the process. Anyone, even D'Acunto, can get an application accepted if he or she files the proper forms.

"Can I say one more thing in closing?" asks Joe, raising his hand for the first time. He launches into a patriotic speech that nobody wants to hear. The chairman cuts him off before someone else does. "You have continued activities at your ranch with the knowledge that you didn't have a legal permit. You have now filed an application for a special-use permit, and we've accepted your application. This meeting is over." And the Rough Rider turns tail and heads for the hills.

Soon after, the Jewett town enforcer heads up to D'Acunto's ranch and orders the Rough Rider to remove his signs and cease all commercial activities until his permits are in order. Notwithstanding, reports persist that D'Acunto is continuing down the same paths with his horses. At a subsequent meeting of the planning board, D'Acunto's application is given a great deal of consideration. This time, however, there is a unanimous vote to reject it. It is currently illegal for D'Acunto to run any kind of a business on his property. The Rough Rider's last recourse is to appeal this decision. Thus far, Virginia City is quiet.

Jams (a.k.a. Hope), a puppy mill survivor

SIX

The Rescue

IT IS EIGHT O'CLOCK in the morning and one of the most bitter Valentine's Days on record. I am bundled up in layers of not-warm-enough clothing, standing in the parking lot of a gas station in Pittstown, New York, just east of Troy. Laura-Ann is with me, and she's shivering so violently that she can't get a sip of hot coffee into her mouth. She is always cold, even in August, so this is torture for her. The snow is coming down in balls of ice that feel like boulders when they hit.

Pittstown isn't what it used to be. The main roads are lined with ranch homes, trailer parks, and a few stately colonials now on the edge of being turned into real estate. This is fast-food country, like the rest of America. A century ago, or even a few decades ago,

I would have been looking at rolling meadows covered with cows or sheep and untouched forests dotted with healthy white birch. Now, I count FOR SALE signs along the roads.

At the moment, everything is covered in two feet of snow, and it's still coming down. Mountainous drifts line the roads, cutting off the views. No one goes out in this weather unless absolutely necessary. Laura-Ann and I are waiting with a group of fourteen unusually committed people—state troopers, dog-control officers, and humane law enforcement agents—all experts in animal cruelty. The puppy mill we're here to raid is just up the hill from this gas station. Part of me is looking forward to seeing what all the fuss over puppy mills is really about. Another part is dreading the experience.

The term "puppy mill" conjures up newspaper headlines, like a recent one in the *New York Post*, which covered a raid on an Amish farm in Pennsylvania: "$4.4M Puppy Mill Scandal." This place had such a high volume of sick dogs, it made the horror stories about the usual busts look like minor skirmishes. I had never really contemplated the potential profit in farming purebred dogs. According to the *Post*, one man in the town of Blue Ball made almost $300,000 in 1995, selling 1,293 puppies. This particular farmer had already won himself a reputation with federal investigators for substandard conditions, including lack of proper food and water for the animals.

Unlike the people who run puppy mills, professional breeders, at least in theory, carefully control and limit the supply of puppies. Their dogs are sold from their homes to people who are screened, to lesser and greater degrees. Many breeders have only one litter every couple of years and do not make a profit; if they break even after the stud fees, medical bills, and general expenses are paid, they are doing well. Chances are, if they show their dogs—and most breeders do—they lose money, given the attendant expenses.

"People generally breed dogs for two reasons," explains Caroline Mouris, who has been breeding wirehaired fox terriers in Columbia County for more than a decade. "They really like the breed and want to improve it, or they treat breeding and showing as a serious sport. The latter group are very competitive, but there are many breeders who fall into both categories." Caroline and her husband, Frank, don't regularly show their dogs. They usually have one litter a year, largely because they love the puppies. But they also strive to improve the breed. "Serious breeders are involved in the genetics," says Caroline. For them, breeding is definitely not a profitable enterprise; the Mourises own four adult terriers who do not pay their own way. (Caroline and Frank are animators, and their work appears on *Sesame Street* and Nickelodeon.) Caroline follows up on every pup she places, making sure that he or she is spayed or neutered and content.

Other breeders, like Charlene Marchand, take showing very seriously. Marchand is totally dedicated to German shepherds, a dominant breed that requires training. Getting a puppy out of Marchand is even more difficult than getting one out of Cammisa. No one gets one of Marchand's shepherds unless they sign a contract requiring them to raise their new pups in the manner in which these dogs have been accustomed to living. They must be fed certain food, properly exercised daily, and put in school. Owners must also be willing to be in constant communication with Marchand. "That's the deal," she explains. "No exceptions."

Marchand and her husband, Michael Wilson, have recently

purchased a new dog, a thirteen-month-old shepherd, whom they are training and physically conditioning to become a star. This process requires a sizable financial investment, the right handler to show the dog in the ring, and a certain amount of social and political savvy. Charlene glows when she talks about Scarlet Letter, the new dog. Indeed, she might be an exquisite example of her breed and may even turn out to be a world-class champion. But to the average person, like myself, she is just a shapely, mostly black shepherd with an affectionate personality. If Scarlet turns out to be a winner, Marchand might breed her to keep the line going. But I suspect that finding a mate who will be good enough for this bitch will be difficult. (Marchand, like many breeders, refers to all female dogs as "bitches.")

Marchand and the Mourises have different goals for their dogs, yet these breeders have tremendous integrity. Unfortunately, backyard breeders—the ones who put ads in newspapers or sell puppies at flea markets—do not, and they are vastly more common. These folks pay less attention to genetics than to their cash flow. People who are in it only for the money have to produce a volume of dogs. Caroline argues that "there are some good breeders who sell a lot of dogs who are not running puppy mills." They are running "kennels," for better or worse, and some of them drop off their puppies at pet stores. But puppy mill breeders are the bottom feeders in this market.

Despite protests and busts organized by organizations like the ASPCA, PETA, and HSUS, most puppy mills operate with impunity. If there's a demand, suppliers prevail. This is why humane societies, purebred rescuers, animal welfare groups, and animal rights organizations are all seeking legislation that would prevent pet stores from selling puppies and kittens. (Enlightened pet stores have already curtailed this end of their business.) Investigators and veterinarians have consistently found that adults taken from puppy mills are undernourished and overbred and their litters are inbred. The puppies are transported in inhumane vehicles to stores and malls where they are frequently sick on arrival with infectious diseases. Thousands of these dogs end up in shelters each year.

This morning's raid has been in the planning stages at the Mohawk and Hudson River Humane Society in Menands, New York, for over a year. It will be spearheaded by Robert Guyer, a cruelty investigator for Rensselaer County, and trooper Sue McDonough, who obtained the search warrant. The date was picked the second they had the warrant, and eight New York State shelters have agreed to help house the animals. There are presently a dozen vans in this Pittstown gas station, their motors purring, waiting to take an unknown number of dogs to safety. One of the vans belongs to the Columbia-Greene Humane Society, and I am driving it. (It is lousy on icy roads.) I am about to see where that cute little doggie in the window of the local pet store comes from.

McDonough, who has the most experience in large raids, is in charge of this operation. She's a thin, blond woman in her midforties, who is dedicated to rescuing animals. Apart from her reputation as a tireless cruelty investigator, she is also a licensed wildlife rehabilitator. "I don't like people very much," she frequently says, only half kidding. "And I only allow dogs and cats to slobber on me."

McDonough and Guyer will go up to the house in the first car to serve Maria Stathacos the warrant. Then, depending on how many animals they find, another van will head up the hill, load up, and leave, then another, and another. The process, which has been carefully planned, is intended to keep Stathacos calm by not overwhelming her with the spectacle of animal ambulances and police vehicles. No one wants her to panic and make the task more difficult. The object is to search the premises, every closet and outbuilding, and remove the animals as quickly as possible. It's difficult, however, to keep a secret in Pittstown. No one knows if Stathacos has been tipped off.

I ask one of the veteran dog-control officers hanging out in the parking lot what he expects to find up the hill. "There's no way to tell until you get there," he tells me. "Sometimes the animals are dead, sometimes the people have cleaned up the place and moved the sickest ones out." Like the rest of the team, he seems surprisingly blasé. I realize that I am the only novice on this mission, the single volunteer who has never been inside a puppy mill.

Despite the cold, my journalistic instincts thaw momentarily, and I run up to McDonough and ask if I can accompany her in the first car up the hill. I want to see Stathacos's face as the trooper hands her the warrant. "Who are you?" she asks me. I tell her that Laura-Ann has brought me along as a volunteer. "I'm a writer," I incautiously add. "No," says McDonough, without missing a beat. "Stathacos may have a weapon. People get dangerous when you take away their animals." She dismisses me abruptly. It's time for her to launch the invasion. "Let's get ready!" she shouts to the fleet as she gets into the driver's seat of her snow-covered police car. "I'll radio back news." Then she and Guyer disappear into the blur of white.

We cannot see what's going on up the hill; the wait is interminable. We're all chatting, drinking coffee out of thermoses, just trying to keep warm. No one can stay outside of their vehicles for more than a few minutes without starting to shake. When the radio in the signal car finally starts crackling, everyone jumps into their cars and forms a single line. "We're in!" shouts one of the officers. Laura-Ann and I edge our way into the procession; we're number two. As soon as we see the vehicle ahead of us drive away from the scene, we move up the hill.

Stathacos's kennel is only minutes away. When the ramshackle place comes into sight, it's surprisingly small. From the outside, it looks like an abandoned junkyard. Piles of debris littering the grounds around the main building are just visible under the snow; I can make out several rusty cages. There's a converted garage and two trailers. An old white horse, flecked with gray, is standing in the falling snow under an open shed. It's not a Hallmark picture.

Laura-Ann and I step out of the van onto the icy ground and take a few awkward, treacherous steps. The muffled sound of barking dogs is immediately audible, like thunder rumbling in the distance, but it's impossible to get a sense of numbers from the noise. We can see Stathacos and McDonough standing in the doorway of her "kennel" talking. Judging from their body language, Stathacos appears to be fully cooperating, but it's hard to know. Her gray hair is short and uncombed, as if she just rolled out of bed. Wearing an old sweatshirt and jeans, she looks unkempt and rumpled, but not angry or out of control.

When we get close, maybe twenty feet from the building, the stench hits and makes me gag. The place stinks of animals, garbage, feces, urine. "We're lucky it's winter," Laura-Ann comments quietly. "Imagine what the place must smell like in the summer."

Laura-Ann is shivering so violently it's difficult for her to speak; her words are vibrating in her throat.

McDonough waves us into the building, right past Stathacos, into a dark area filled with cages. The staccato barking and whimpering is like a deranged opera sung by hysterics. The reek is overwhelming. I pull my scarf up over my mouth, somewhat self-consciously. But I notice others have done the same. Our task is to fill our van with dogs and drive them to the Mohawk and Hudson River shelter, the closest facility, where a team of veterinarians, all volunteers, is waiting to examine each animal. There is one vet, Kate Adsit, at the scene. Laura-Ann and I are lugging four carriers; we have eight more in the car.

It is so dark in Stathacos's shed that at first I cannot see very much. There are no windows nor running water; someone has hooked up a few makeshift lights, but there is no heat. The air is thick and stale. The floor is covered with several inches of dirt, feces, hair—who knows?—it feels squishy under our boots. As my eyes adjust to the darkness, I peek into a room stacked with cages that are crammed with dogs. The animals are barking furiously. No one has done a head count because it's impossible to see how many are stuffed into each cage. McDonough wants us to go in and remove the dogs, cage by cage, room by room; she is numbering and photographing them as they go out the door, never to return—we hope.

Laura-Ann and I move cautiously into the main area, a narrow room, maybe fifty by twenty feet, stacked with two-by-two-foot cages that are filled with yapping small dogs; most contain five or six of them. I notice Yorkshire terriers, West Highland terriers, cairn terriers, poodles, and dachshunds. There aren't many puppies, but there are dozens of older dogs and pregnant females.

Kelly Collins and Cathy Crawmer are overseeing the transfer of the animals from their cages to the carriers that will take them to safety. Collins is another trainer and also a local Labrador retriever rescuer, which means she takes in abandoned purebred Labs, works with them, and eventually places them in homes. I watch Collins stick her long arm into Stathacos's filthy cages and attempt to pull out the dogs, one by one. Sometimes, she doesn't know what's going to come out. The problem is that many of the dogs are stuck together because they have been defecating on each other; stacking cages allows feces and urine to drip into the cage below. The dogs have not been groomed in months, years, or maybe ever. The longhairs are the worst off. Their coats are matted into dreadlocks. Many of them can't see because their hair has grown over their eyes and become tangled in dense masses. These dogs have been living in darkness. What I can't understand is how they have the energy to bark so frantically.

On one side of the room, there are three or four larger crates filled with Great Danes. The dogs look relatively young, and they are all lying down. Then I realize that their cages are so small they might be uncomfortable standing up.

I find it hard to believe, but Stathacos is able to register puppies born in this "kennel" with the American Kennel Club. Many of her dogs are sold with official certificates from the most prestigious purebred dog registry in the country. This piece of paper, not unlike a Good Housekeeping Seal of Approval on a toaster, is critical to the consumer's confidence in the product. Most pet-store pups come with AKC papers, which I had naively assumed, until now, meant they came from quality breeders. But the AKC monitors their paperwork, not their kennels or dogs.

Everyone is in high gear, silently loading the dogs into carriers. There is acknowledgment of the degradation exclusively through eye contact and careful glances, not words. "Don't respond," Laura-Ann whispers to me. "Concentrate on getting the dogs out." She is my guide, keeping me moving when I stop and stare in disbelief.

Collins is stuffing two poodles into one of my carriers. I walk them to the car, take a breath of fresh air, and go back for more. When Laura-Ann and I have loaded twelve carriers of dogs into our van and we are ready to leave, McDonough grabs us, hands Laura-Ann a flashlight, and says, "Go downstairs and get a head count." I didn't even realize there was a downstairs.

Laura-Ann takes me to a dark corner where a makeshift set of plywood steps leads down to the basement. Now, I hear the dogs downstairs. It's pitch black, and I hesitate. Laura-Ann senses my fear and immediately takes the lead. "I've seen it all," she says to me quietly. Then she carefully makes her way down the stairs, clearing away cobwebs, and with flashlight in hand, enters a lightless room filled with the sound of dogs.

When the flashlight goes on, casting a dim beam into the space, we are faced with a makeshift pen holding about twenty small dogs, including a mother and her nursing pups. It's difficult to count them because they are all squirming to get near us. I see a white dog with a bunch of teeny pups, just days old, drinking from her belly. I assume the dogs were too young to sell off before our arrival. The mother dog has a look of terror in her eyes. I reach into the pen to let a few frenzied poodles smell my hand, really my glove. (Never offer a strange dog the palm of your hand or individual fingers;

make a fist and let the dog sniff the back of the hand.) They swarm around it, like bees, but when I bend down to get closer, they scatter. There's no food or water anywhere in sight.

When I look up, Laura-Ann is gone. She is counting heads, doing the work that needs to get done. There's a hallway leading to the larger part of the basement. She calls for me, shining her flashlight through a narrow passageway lined by rows of floor-to-ceiling cages that connects to the larger part of the basement. The dogs bark and lunge at me as I walk through this narrow space. It's like being in a horror movie. It's difficult to tell if these dogs are aggressive or just frantic. Stathacos was keeping larger dogs in the basement.

As we go through, many of them bounce up and down in their cages as if they have gone stark-raving mad. When Laura Ann shines a light into the back of one of the cages, I see some smaller, older dogs. Many are lying down. They are too old, too depressed, or too sick to get excited. There are several Danes, one very distinct bull terrier, cocker spaniels, an elderly brindled pit bull, groups of dogs who must have been living in this subterranean inferno for untold years. They are matted, covered with feces, thin, blind, old. There's a cocker in the back of one cage with piercing blue eyes who is completely still, just sitting quietly.

Laura-Ann tells me to count the dogs in the area and keep moving. There are eighty-seven dogs in this dungeon. "They're all alive," she says. "It could be worse."

We go upstairs to report to McDonough, who is standing with Stathacos. She is calmly observing the proceedings, not showing any emotion or acknowledging individual dogs as they leave. I keep thinking that she must be masking her feelings, that she must be terribly upset about all of this. But it is hard to know. She is watching her livelihood march out the door, not her pets. "There goes a thousand dollars," she comments as a particularly cute dachshund gets carried away. She must have known we were coming. There are too few puppies around, so the assumption is that she either hid them or sold them.

I would like to speak with Stathacos, to find out if she has an explanation for the state of her kennel, but McDonough won't allow any of us to talk with the woman. The trooper is guarding her prey like a hawk, chatting her up, and offering her reassurance that every one of her dogs is going to receive excellent care at various shelters all over the state. As I walk out of the building for the last time, I overhear Stathacos say, with some relief, "There sure are a lot of animals in here. Why don't you people lose a few." McDonough doesn't respond.

Outside, two shelter people are carrying a large Dane to their van; the dog either won't, or can't, walk. She seems frozen with fear. When they pass me, I can't help but notice that the Dane is squinting. I wonder if this dog has ever seen daylight.

The snow is still falling as Laura-Ann and I make the forty-five-minute drive to the Mohawk shelter with our vanload of animals. We are both exhausted. Neither of us has eaten all day; neither of us is hungry. The immediate goal is to get these animals checked by a vet and out of our cramped carriers. To our surprise, the dogs are quiet in the car, a little too quiet. While I drive, Laura-Ann talks to them, peeking into each carrier to make sure they're OK. When a poor little Westie who is covered with crusty knots vomits, we pull over to clean her up. Without water, it's a futile task.

The Mohawk shelter looks like an emergency room after a disaster: It's filled with animals, cages, and blankets. There's a line of dog-control officers with dogs waiting to get in to see the vets. Someone says the head count in the shelter is already over a hundred. A team of three doctors (including Holly Cheever, a well-known activist veterinarian) examines each dog for about five minutes each; the animals are assessed, written up on charts, and are vaccinated for distemper and parvo. It is a relief to see these dogs getting medical attention. None have been given any water or food for hours. After their examinations, they are put in cages with water; food will come later, after they calm down a little.

What is immediately striking is how unsocialized these dogs are. Many of them seem catatonic. They do not respond to human attention. This is not the case with some of the small terriers and poodles who are frantic in their cages. The vets are finding tumors, infections, eye and teeth problems, skin diseases, pneumonia, and a variety of ailments—the ravages of bad breeding, poor nutrition, overcrowding, and lack of adequate grooming. Fifteen dogs are in such terrible condition that they are euthanized immediately.

As I walk past the euthanasia room, I recognize the old cocker with the piercing blue eyes from the basement, her coat wet from the snow. Up close, I can see that she has cataracts; both her eyes are covered with a milky liquid, as if they are melting in her head. The dog is so old and arthritic, she's virtually unable to move. My immediate instinct is to rush in to tell them I will take this dog home, but instead I stand quietly and watch her take her final breaths. There's a euthanasia technician holding the old dog in her arms, stroking her head and talking to her as she injects a lethal dose of sodium pentothal into a vein in her paw. Within ten seconds, the old dog is dead. I feel like a part of me has died with her.

When Collins walks by holding a limp cairn terrier in her arms, I recognize the dog. Laura-Ann and I carried her in our van. "What happened to her?" I ask. Collins looks at me strangely. "Are you kidding?" she asks. The dog has just been euthanized and is on the way to the cold room. A limp corpse is an easily recognizable sight for most of the people on this mission.

I have to get out, so I go sit in the van for a while. But there's nowhere to hide; ambulances full of dogs are still pulling into the shelter. Laura-Ann appears in the doorway and shouts at me to come back inside. "It's time to pick out some dogs to bring back to Columbia-Greene," she informs me. She wants to take ten to fifteen small dogs, which will take up about four runs. Laura-Ann wants females, so they can be grouped together without risk of pregnancy. "You pick," she adds. "It's all the same to me."

Selecting the animals seems like a major task to leave up to me. "Don't you want a say in it?" I ask.

"Not really," says the director. I can tell that she is bone tired of these situations.

"But do I take the most adoptable dogs, the youngest ones, the sickest, or some of each? What's fair?"

Laura-Ann advises me to select animals who will not need significant medical attention. She reminds me that the shelter is broke and the staff has little time to care for sick animals. I suddenly realize what a burden these dogs are going to be, yet the director is determined to help. "I bet you already have some dogs picked out," Cammisa adds. She's right, again.

"Remember the West Highland terrier covered in mats? She's a female," I tell Laura-Ann, walking her over to the dog's cage. The dog still looks unhappy, but she is now in the company of a younger Westie, who looks a little healthier. "She's older, but she passed the vet inspection with no major problems," I tell Laura-Ann. "Fine," she responds. "Take them both."

Nearby, there are a group of three active miniature poodles. I can't tell their ages, but they look like adults and have been vaccinated; I decide to take them all, largely because I can't choose among them. A shelter worker walks through the kennel holding a large carrier containing a nursing mother and her litter. "Who will take these dogs?" he shouts, as if this were an auction. The carrier is so big and heavy that he wants to put it directly into a vehicle. I recognize her right away; it's the white dog from the basement and all her pups. I already feel a connection to this group, so I direct him to our vehicle.

Laura-Ann is watching me, showing some concern for the rationale behind this choice. "Do I have to count the six babies among the fifteen dogs we take?" I ask her. "Of course," she says. "Babies grow up. You're going to get to know every one of them. This case could take months, even years, to settle." Reality is settling in.

Three more dogs to go. I feel like a kid in a candy store. Instead of going for the neediest cases, I decide to grab two healthy little Yorkies and an adorable schnauzer-poodle (a schnoodle?) who must have been part of an accidental litter. There are few mutts in this crowd.

But there's still one dog I want to find. I ask around if anyone has seen the bull terrier from Stathacos's basement. There are already fifteen dogs in the van, so I'm wondering if I can talk Laura-Ann into taking one more. But I can't find the dog. I've checked everywhere but the euthanasia room, and I don't want to go back there. Then I spot her! The dog is wrapped in Sue McDonough's arms as she walks into the shelter, the last person and dog to exit the scene. "Isn't she cute?" the trooper says insistently. McDonough has a wicked crush on the dog. It's about five o'clock, and she is elated, running on adrenaline. Most of the people involved in this mission have chosen a particular animal to focus on, to save personally. For McDonough, it's this bull terrier. For me, it's the white mother, and I've got her safely in the shelter van.

McDonough informs everyone that all the animals, with the exception of the horse, have been removed from Stathacos's home. There's an exhausted cheer from the whole group, and then the vets go back to work. Some people are disappointed about the horse. "The horse was healthy," McDonough insists, "We couldn't legally take it. It had shelter and food."

Stathacos has been charged with one hundred counts of cruelty to animals; 138 dogs have been removed from the premises. (Joel Abelove, the district attorney for Rensselaer County, who is prosecuting the case, has advised McDonough to press charges on only the sickest animals.) "When I left," says McDonough, "Maria was giving an interview to a television crew, telling them that she intends to get every one of her dogs back." The trooper shrewdly invited the press to come over to the shelter and see the dogs for themselves—right away. One hour later, the press arrives, and their footage makes it onto the eleven o'clock news that night. The same footage will be shown again, nine months later, in a courtroom.

"Has anybody ordered pizza?" shouts McDonough, still clutching her dog. Everybody laughs, relaxes for a moment, and recognizes their collective hunger. No one has ordered pizza.

Laura-Ann and I head back to Columbia-Greene with the dogs. When we leave, there are still animals sitting in vans, in hallways, in offices, waiting for their exams. The drive back to Hudson, about an hour, is quiet. There are a few whimpers from the babies and some more vomiting, but the dogs are mostly silent. By nine o'clock, they are settled into clean, indoor/outdoor kennels. Each dog has a blanket, a bowl of food, and water. I wonder if the cold cement floors of this shelter feel like the Ritz to this group.

A little white poodle is named Valentine, to commemorate the day of the raid. The white mother dog (actually a spitz), whom we name Spirit, gobbles up her dinner as if she were starving. But she is nursing, so she is given a second bowl. None of the others can have too much too quickly, or they will become sick. The poodles collapse in fatigue, maybe fear. The two Westies (Hope and Grace) fight over their food and must be separated to eat; Hope, the matted rasta-Westie, is completely submissive. The fetching little Yorkies (Button and Thimble) are the most frazzled members of the Pittstown group. They can't stop shaking.

The dogs who are already in residence at Columbia-Greene bark fiercely at the newcomers as they enter their new home. There's a pecking order in the shelter, mostly determined by seniority. The puppy mill dogs will be in residence for months. Soon they will be the top dogs, treating newcomers with the same ferocity that they are welcomed with tonight.

———

THE PITTSTOWN fifteen come to personify the shelter's mission with an almost religious passion, signifying both the misery that animals endure and the possibility of redemption. The dogs become local celebrities as the project of their rehabilitation is embraced by the press and the community. Photographers, ministers, trainers, dog-food companies, groomers, schoolchildren, and senior citizens come to the shelter with offerings of blankets, food, and money. People volunteer hours of their time to sit and hold the dogs in an effort to teach them to trust human beings.

This is a complex process. The dogs have myriad problems, many of which, in the drama of the moment, were completely undiscernible to the veterinarians and rescuers alike. Valentine is pregnant and gives birth to one stillborn puppy. Two from Spirit's litter die within weeks, but the others begin to revive right away. Oddly enough, they turn out to be accidental mutts, terrier mixes, who have the dubious pleasure of growing up in the shelter. Hope, the older Westie, has tumors and a hernia; she requires immediate surgery. Grace, the younger one, is frightened of people. None of the dogs are housebroken; none seem to have ever been on a leash or, for that matter, inside a home. The poodles and Westies require constant grooming therapy to acclimate them to the process and to people. There are lists of people waiting to adopt the dogs. The goal is to get them out of the shelter and into homes as soon as possible.

But getting an animal-cruelty case into a small-town courtroom requires reservoirs of patience. As the dogs remain incarcerated, month after month, I remind myself that, at the very least, none of them know what they are missing. Stathacos argues, whenever the press listens, that she is a reputable breeder. The woman still wants every one of her dogs back. Her lawyer claims that she is in compliance with all state regulations and federal standards for animals. But Stathacos and this lawyer part ways and it takes some time before she gets a new one. Her next hurdle is a change of venue.

Meanwhile, the dogs are taking up space in shelters all over upstate New York. After they have been housed for almost five months, and there is no trial date in sight, Laura-Ann decides to find foster homes. Her board is nervous, but the director insists. She needs the kennel space, and the dogs are getting stir-crazy. They need to be moved into real homes to begin the difficult transition into becoming house pets. A newspaper article reports that the Mohawk and Hudson River shelter has euthanized forty dogs to make room for the Pittstown crowd; Mohawk is holding sixty of Stathacos's dogs. At this point, many of the shelters decide to foster out the dogs before the deaths mount further.

FINALLY, nine months later, Laura-Ann and I are sitting in a courtroom, which is located in the middle of a field. The case has been moved to Schaghticoke, New York, northwest of Pittstown. We are not here by choice; both of us have been subpoenaed to appear for the defendant. I can't imagine why Stathacos would want to give either one of us the opportunity to wax eloquent on the virtues of puppy mills. Her lawyer does not greet us or interview us. Instead, a bailiff sends us to an alcove where we spend the day watching various character witnesses go in and out of the courtroom to testify on behalf of Stathacos. One of them, according to a subsequent newspaper account, suggests that a videotape made after the seizure that shows a group of pitiful dogs being groomed might have been set up. I imagine a brilliant team of makeup artists coming into the shelter to work on these dogs.

Toward the end of the day, Cammisa is called to testify but I don't have this pleasure. As it turns out, her attorney misspelled my name, so technically, as the district attorney points out to the judge, I do not exist.

The trial proceeds in a way that Cammisa describes as "usual for cruelty cases." The attorney puts McDonough on the stand, for instance, and paints her as a rabid vegetable eater and animal rights activist with an ideological agenda. "Are you a member of PETA?" he asks her, as if it were a Communist organization. I wonder what the jury thinks about animal rights. If they have pets, then just watching the videotape should have put them on the side of the Humane Society. But if they have fur coats in their closets, then they might be a little nervous about PETA.

Actually, I have my grandmother's coat (black seal) in my closet. But should Stathacos's attorney be intelligent enough to ask me, for instance, if I would walk down the street wearing the coat, I might be in trouble. I also subscribe to PETA's magazine. The publication is a colorful, opinionated compilation of articles and pictures about the atrocious treatment of animals on factory farms, in slaughterhouses, and in research laboratories. It champions those who save animals and promotes the products of companies that have stopped testing on them. PETA actually deserves the credit for initially exposing what goes on inside puppy mills, just like the one that Stathacos is running.

The trial drags on as Stathacos puts crony after crony, breeder after breeder, on the stand to testify to the high quality of care dogs received under her auspices. These breeders are the kind of people from whom one would not want to buy a used car, let alone a puppy. I suspect that Stathacos's attorney is trying to put a mountain of praise in between his client and the images on the videotapes of her dogs. But the jury members have been raised on a diet that includes *Court TV* and *Law & Order.* I'm betting they can identify the villain in the room.

McDonough, who sits in the courthouse day after day, is growing weary and nervous, a state which proves to be productive. While Stathacos's parade of witnesses indiscriminately praises her generosity toward her animals, the trooper notices the conspicuous absence of Stathacos's own vet, the person who actually cared for them over the years. The man is on the witness list, but for some reason he has not been called to testify. Abelove, the district attorney, asks McDonough to give the veterinarian a call.

"I was just chatting with him," McDonough tells me the day before the trial comes to a thunderous climax. "I told him, 'I just want to get your professional opinion on those damn dogs. How did they really look to you?' So he says, 'They looked fine. But puppies usually look fine.'

"I said, 'No, not the puppies, but the adult dogs,' and he says, 'Well, I never saw them.'" Fireworks went off in the trooper's head. "He only vaccinated her puppies!" she shouts with joy.

Tucked safely away in the courtroom, as we speak, are forty-nine rabies certificates, each ostensibly signed by Stathacos's veterinarian, that she has turned in to the judge as evidence. Every one of them is a forgery. Maria Stathacos is a dead duck.

It takes the jury only a few hours to convict her of fifty-seven counts (some are dropped on technicalities) of animal abuse. No one is surprised except Stathacos. Soon after, the judge sentences her to four months in jail, orders her to pay the Mohawk and Hudson River shelter $65,000 in restitution, and forbids her to have any dogs in her possession for the next ten years.

When I bump into Bob Guyer almost one year later, he tells me that Stathacos is out of jail, selling chickens, guinea hens, goats, and pigs. There was nothing in the judge's sentence to prevent her from raising or selling livestock. "She hasn't paid a dime of the money she owes us," he adds. Guyer intends to serve her a summons to get her back into court again.

Jitters, whose good manners saved his life

SEVEN

The Last Resort

My neighbors, Charlie and Brenda, stop by to show me a stray who has been hanging around their house all morning. "Do you know him?" Charlie asks, hoping I might be able to identify the dog. They are debating whether or not to keep him. The dog, the color of cream, has big brown eyes and a jet black nose. He looks under a year, but aging a dog is not an exact science. (All you can do is check the sharpness of the teeth and the amount of tartar.) His ears are up, suggesting shepherd in the mix, yet he's small and stout, more the shape of a husky. His tongue is splattered with drippy blue spots and streaks like a Jackson Pollock.

I don't recognize this dog, but other neighbors have called to complain about a white dog, who they assumed was Snowy, running through their flower beds. Snowy, however, has been falsely accused. She is generally either at my side or sitting in front of the house. I realize that I am face-to-face with the culprit who has been tainting my own dog's reputation. They're almost the same color.

The mystery dog is an easygoing, happy-go-lucky type, willing to go anywhere, do anything. He follows Snowy around like a duckling. Snowy likes him; he's submissive. The dogs play and tumble like best friends. Kate, no surprise, falls instantly in love. Even Peter, my husband, likes him. Charlie and Brenda, thank goodness, want to give the dog a home.

"Go house to house and you'll find his owner," I advise them. "I bet they'll be happy to *give* you this dog. Whoever it is seems to be letting him stray." They take the dog and leave.

The next morning, I get a wake-up call from Charlie. They found the owner of the dog, who says he is an eight-month-old cross between a husky and a Great Pyrenees. The owner readily gave the dog to his finder. Now Charlie and Brenda have a different problem. The dog kept them awake all night, and their eight-year-old Ibizan hound is beside herself. They don't want to return the dog to his original owner—too many rottweilers for comfort. "Please take him to the shelter," Charlie begs me.

Kate and I go get the dog. Charlie brings him out, and he hops into the car as if he's been riding with us his whole life. He sits on the floor at Kate's feet with his head cradled in her lap. My daughter is silent for most of the ride, but as we turn down Humane Society Road, she says, "That's it. We can't do this."

After watching hundreds of people bring in their dogs, I should have anticipated Kate's reaction. I remind her that I have resisted taking home countless dogs from the shelter while writing this book in an attempt to keep our own pet population down to a reasonable number. At the moment, we commute between the city and the country in a car packed with three people, one dog, one cat, and two computers; the family is already verging on becoming a vaudeville act. We cannot keep this dog, whom we've known for less than twenty-four hours.

"What if no one wants him? What if he's euthanized?" Kate asks, getting right to the heart of the matter. Then she begins to weep. "Let's just take him home," she pleads. "I promise I'll take care of him." This line does not work on me at all. I tell Kate several times that I will watch over the fate of this dog in the shelter. But there is no consoling her. We both know the drill. The truth is, I'm not just giving this dog a lift to the pound, I'm surrendering him to a shelter where he might be euthanized for one of any number of reasons.

I pull into the driveway with a sick feeling in my stomach. I decide to take the dog into the kennel myself and set him up with food, water, and a blanket. I wonder what name he will be given. There's a sadness that accompanies dogs who arrive nameless, and I've just delivered one. The other residents are barking and growling, as usual. My nameless friend starts vibrating with fear. This is the first time I have seen him show any anxiety.

This place, which I know so well, suddenly looks very different and very scary. I am wondering if I can bear to watch strangers come and go through the kennels and pass up this sweet, harmless dog. Can I really protect him? Thus far, I'm not doing such a great job. Yesterday he was something special. Today he's just another anonymous mutt at the pound.

The dog is quivering in his cage, and Kate is crying in the car.

I have become one of the characters in my own book, having difficulty parting with a dog. I remember Kate Meehan, a trainer who
was once on the board of directors, giving me a piece of advice:
"Don't bring an animal here yourself unless you are ready to let go.
Once they are in the shelter, you have no more say." She was absolutely right. I have to be willing to allow the shelter to either
place or euthanize this dog. Moreover, I have to trust that Cammisa will do the right thing. But what if she's on vacation? (She
never takes vacations.) What if the dog gets sick? Is it fair to request special treatment for him and put others at risk?

I return to the car to talk to Kate, but there is no reason to say
anything. She has watched me comfort others and then seen their
dogs and cats get put down. We both know how many animals
there are and how little justice there is for them. Animals are killed
because they are vicious or sick; but beyond that, shelters play
Russian roulette with their lives. Their fates are unduly influenced
by the public's whims. People who watch *Frasier* want Jack Russell
terriers, and children who have been to Neverland want shaggy
sheepdogs. All the kids want dalmatians instead of, or in addition
to, the pets they have already.

Ultimately, animals are penalized in shelters because they do
not meet market standards set by animal lovers, pet stores, and cul-
tural fantasies of ideal pets. At the moment, carrying a miniature
pinscher or a Yorkshire terrier around in a purse is considered chic
in some circles; entrance into another social group requires a pit
bull brutally trained to take punishment and fight until death. Dogs
that don't happen to be trendy don't get adopted, and the longer
they stay at the shelter, the harder they are to place. Time after time,
the dogs and cats with the optimum temperaments get overlooked

for months at Columbia-Greene because people are suspicious of the animals who have been there the longest. What they don't realize is that these animals are frequently the best ones; their immune systems are solid, and they are able to adjust to stressful conditions. These are two important qualities to have in a pet.

Cammisa spends her days looking for reasons to choose animals for euthanasia and her nights obsessively loving the ones she saves. This is what people are trained to do in the animal welfare movement. But there is something deeply flawed with this system, and even the animals' most dedicated advocates have not been able to fix it.

"I can't do this, either," I admit to Kate. "Let's go get him." She lights up from within and starts breathing again. Together, we walk back into the kennel, take our dog out of the cage, and bring him home. His name is Tramp (after Charlie Chaplin), and as I write, he is sleeping beneath my desk.

MY EXPERIENCE with Tramp makes me realize that I have avoided facing the reality of euthanasia, just like the rest of the public. In part, this is because Cammisa, like most shelter directors, plays down the fact of euthanasia to protect the animals in her care from controversy. No one likes to think about all the dogs and cats who are sentenced to death without having committed any crime. "When the media launches an attack, adoption rates go down, and euthanasia goes up," says the director. "It only hurts the animals." She has lived through several clashes with the press. One summer, a disgruntled board member resigned, went to the local paper, and complained that the shelter unnecessarily euthanized animals. Cammisa was philosophical about this debacle. She says gloomily, "It goes with the territory."

As a result of publicity like this, the shelter rarely initiates public discussions on euthanasia. If people ask about the shelter's policies, they are given a nutshell version of what is essentially a process of triage. But most people never ask because they don't want to know. Columbia-Greene informs surrenderers when their animals are adopted, but there's no follow-up call when the animals are killed. People want happy endings or none at all. They say their good-byes at the shelter door, which is hard enough. After that, the animal's fate is on the shelter's conscience.

Nationwide, shelter employees suffer from a collective depression. Who can blame them? Altogether, according to PETA, they euthanize more than thirty thousand animals each day. These animals are not eaten, trapped for their fur, or sent to research laboratories. They are unwanted pets, prematurely transformed into smoke and ash. When I first smelled the crematory at Columbia-Greene, I thought the whole place was on fire. Eventually everyone learns to live with this odor. But I knew a time would come when I would also have to feel the heat.

One morning in August, I get a call from Laura-Ann because three people are out with the flu; she needs help. When I get there, the director is in the back loading the crematory alone. The night before, thirty-seven sickly animals were taken from a collector; thirty-six were immediately euthanized. (The single survivor is a blue point Siamese kitten.) The cold room is so full of bodies that the furnace will have to run all day long. Laura-Ann emerges wearing rubber gloves and asks if I will help her load up the crematory.

I reluctantly agree. The director senses my resistance, but she wants me to go in and see the bodies, to witness the appalling reality of unwanted animals. None of the board members has been in the cold room. Even some of the shelter employees refuse to go in; they want no part of the killing process. This makes Laura-Ann extremely uncomfortable. She wants everyone to understand and participate in the euthanasia work. "Otherwise the staff becomes divided between the murderers and the saviors," she explains.

The cold room is dark, smaller and more macabre than I imagined. There are piles of bodies on the floor. Laura-Ann marches right in, grabbing two cats by their legs, one corpse in each hand. "It's easier to get them into the crematory before rigor mortis sets in," she tells me. "You can get more of them in at one time."

There's a huge, swollen dalmatian, wearing a bright blue collar, on the top of a heap of dogs. It's a dog I've never seen.

"Whose dog is that?" I ask.

"She came over from the Athens shelter—vicious," the director explains.

"Shouldn't we take off their collars?" I ask. "Not yet," she says. "It's easier to carry them by the collars." We lift the dalmatian together into the crematory. I'm moving in slow motion, while Laura-Ann swiftly moves back and forth between the cold room and the crematory. It's as if she were cleaning out her garage.

I can't stop staring at the piles. I suddenly recognize a Lab named Jake, placed and returned. Then I see Bandit, the Akita-dalmatian mix—everyone's favorite dog. The pile is coming alive for me as I begin to identify animals. I've been around the shelter for almost two years, and I have read the euthanasia statistics, voiced opinions on whether animals were adoptable or not, and come to understand why some must die so others can live. But I never witnessed the stone-cold impact of these decisions. I'm frozen, too.

"Look," Laura-Ann says graciously. "It doesn't bother me. Really. You can leave. I've done this alone for years." I decide to get some air.

AT FIRST, I was using the term "put to sleep" to describe the end result of euthanasia. One afternoon at the shelter, Dr. Tatty Hodge, a veterinarian who is putting down a litter of puppies with parvo, hears me utter this euphemism. "Wipe that out of your vernacular," she says. "Unless you really believe these animals are going to wake up again."

They don't wake up. But I woke up. I stopped asking questions and began checking the paperwork myself to find out who lived and who died. Eventually I began to do the math and joined the staff in its frantic efforts to place animals who were about to be killed. Once I was more involved, Laura-Ann pushed me about euthanasia. Would I do it? How do I feel about it? She is always looking for people who might be willing to take the training. I won't. But I do agree with her that every unwanted animal deserves a humane death. The problem is that this privilege is largely given to healthy, adoptable animals. She doesn't disagree. Who could?

Friday is usually euthanasia day. Shelters with veterinarians on staff can put animals down any day of the week, but Columbia-Greene relies mostly on volunteers. Finding people to do the task is always a problem. One woman, a licensed technician, euthanized shelter animals for more than five years and totally burned out; she became depressed and angry. Toward the end, if a staff member questioned her about a euthanasia decision, she would burst into tears. She finally quit.

Euthanizing animals, especially in large numbers, is a demanding, highly skilled activity. Humane organizations offer workshops and conferences where new techniques, drugs, and skills are shared and debated. There are different ways, for instance, to hold animals during this process. Some technicians like to place them up on tables; others insist on getting down on the floor with the animals. Medical issues determine whether the animals are injected in their legs, or directly into their hearts. Some people like to tranquilize first; others won't because the animals frequently vomit. Technicians exchange shoptalk about the quickest way to find an adequate vein.

One Friday at the shelter, Sue McDonough volunteers her time euthanizing animals. Her attitude is businesslike; the work needs to be done, and she wants to be able to put suffering animals out of their misery. After a short period, she comes marching out of the euthanasia room with a buff-colored cocker spaniel. "I'm not euthanizing this dog," she announces. "I put him on the table, and he handed me his paw. I don't kill animals who want to shake my hand first." If McDonough doesn't want to kill the dog, so be it.

The cocker was found in a storm tethered to a lamppost. A woman heard him whimpering early in the morning and brought him to the shelter half frozen. He had been sitting in the back of his kennel, shaking violently, for five days. The staff named him Jitters. Jitters became Jangles and was adopted his first day in the main kennel. I called his new owners one week later. I couldn't get them off the phone; they worship the dog.

When Laura-Ann makes euthanasia rounds, the staff gets

moody and upset. For the first time, I decide to accompany her as she makes the final decisions on cats. She frequently does this alone, or with the kennel manager, Sue Pesano. The power in every shelter ultimately lies with the person who has the authority to determine who lives and who dies. Laura-Ann is anxious to share this power with Pesano. "I'm tired of being the grim reaper," she tells us both. Cammisa is burning out. Unlike Andrea Walker, Pesano is not overly sympathetic to abused animals; she's not looking for any rehabilitation challenges. Laura-Ann is pushing to make final decisions earlier rather than later after the staff has become attached to the animals. There is nothing more depressing for kennel workers than feeding and caring for animals and then losing them; this is one reason why people quit.

Pesano has separated out two litters that are completely charming. "They're a little young," says the director right away, frowning. All kittens under six weeks are supposed to be euthanized. "I know they're young," Pesano responds confidently. "But they're healthier than the others," referring to four nearby litters (fifteen kittens) that are scheduled for euthanasia because they are either too young, sick, or were simply born the wrong color. People don't realize that kittens are so plentiful that they are frequently selected for euthanasia on the basis of their color. Black cats, for instance, are more common than calicos; if there are already three black cats up for adoption and a new one arrives, he or she might not even be given a chance. One sneeze can get a cat euthanized rather than medicated if there's a full house.

The mothers of these litters will all be put up for adoption; two of them look about six months old. These are babies having babies, just like teenagers are doing across the country. Laura-Ann picks out two kittens from one of the litters scheduled for euthanasia to save. (Now, only thirteen will die.) "Selecting from a litter is one of the hardest things for me," she says, grabbing two by the scruff of the neck, almost without looking. She is concerned, as always, about the balance of ages in her main adoption rooms. Once the cats make it there, if they remain healthy and content, they stay for months until they are placed. "I wish I could give everybody a chance," she says. "But it's wishful thinking."

There's a longhaired tiger that is absolutely gorgeous who arrived two days ago. The cat is an older unneutered stray, maybe three or four. Pesano has been spending every free minute picking ticks and fleas off of him, but he's still infested. His hair is matted, and he's also got the beginning of some sort of skin problem. He's an obvious candidate for euthanasia because he requires staff time and medical attention. Laura-Ann opens his cage to talk to him, rub his back, and check out his personality. He rolls over for her like a dog, responding to her every touch, and begins purring like a machine. He allows her to dig through his fur and check his skin, his nails, and even his ears. Pesano looks at me and raises her eyes; she's completely smitten. We are both hoping this Tom, Dick, or Harry passes inspection.

"Let's name him Sylvester and get him into the adoption room as soon as possible," says the director as she closes his cage.

A young gray-and-white cat, friendly as can be, doesn't do as well. She's pregnant. Pregnant cats are the most controversial animals at Columbia-Greene, where they are aborted or euthanized, depending on time, space, money, and available veterinarians. Cammisa does not allow any animal to give birth in her shelter.

"Why should I add to the population crisis?" she states flatly. "It wouldn't make sense."

"But does killing them because they are pregnant make sense?" I ask.

"We have no choice. What *should* I do with them?" the director replies. A Catholic ex-staffer told me, "I was very much against abortion when I began working here. But why should a mother have to go through birth just to lose her kittens? I changed my views."

At the Columbia-Greene Humane Society, there's only a modicum of justice for the animals, yet this shelter is infinitely more humane than others, where the immutable criterion is how long an animal has been held. My friend Karen Harris walked into the Center for Animal Care and Control in New York City and fell for a red dog. Karen is an artist and an animal activist; Gus, her vizsla, is spoiled rotten. Karen's husband was not with her, and she asked the CACC adoption counselor if she could return with him the following day; she wanted him to be part of the decision process. But the shelter refused to hold the dog another day. If she wanted him, she had to take him *now*. In Cammisa's shelter, Karen wouldn't get the dog *unless* her husband returned to see him.

There is no code of standard practices that governs adoption or euthanasia policies in this field. National organizations offer shelters advice, materials, training, and assessments of their facilities. (HSUS, founded in 1954, has more than 5 million members.) But each shelter is an independent organization, more accountable to its own local community than any national institution. At the moment, a war is raging over euthanasia. A lot of shelters are getting out of this end of the business altogether and leaving the task to others. Becoming a "no-kill" shelter, as they are called, helps raise funds and wins friends in the community. People want the comfort of giving their animals up to facilities that will not kill them. The question is what quality of life they have, living year after year in cages.

No-kill shelters, unlike Columbia-Greene, do not open their doors to every animal. These facilities pick and choose who they invite in and maintain waiting lists. Young adoptable animals are the most desirable clients for every shelter because they come in and go out quickly. No-kill facilities often refuse animals altogether, leaving them in their owners' hands. Ironically, those most in need are sometimes turned away. When a shelter in Ulster County, on the west side of the Hudson River, recently stopped euthanizing and began refusing surrenders, Columbia-Greene had to deal with the overflow.

When shelters turn animals away, people look for alternatives. Large urban shelters, which take in thousands of animals, can't turn any away unless the city has set up an alternative program and there's a place for them to go. In New York City, for instance, the ASPCA quit doing the job of animal control (collection and euthanasia) for the city and became a no-kill operation, focusing on adoption, education, and cruelty. This forced authorities to create a new agency to do the other work. When one shelter stops routine euthanasia, another must pick up the slack.

"Those of us who run no-kill facilities would be swamped if no one was out there doing euthanasia," admits Sara Whalen. "I just can't do it myself." Whalen runs Pets Alive, a sanctuary for animals in Middletown, New York, that operates at full capacity. She is extremely knowledgeable about animals, the public, and shelter issues. Without blinking an eye, Whalen refuses certain animals altogether, boards some elsewhere until she has an opening, and keeps a waiting list. Her kennel is not open to the public, but she adopts animals out by appointment. Getting through Whalen's screening process is tougher than threading the proverbial needle. If she doesn't like the message on a potential adopter's answering machine, she will end the interview process before it even begins. People call Whalen when there is an animal in trouble; she is known for her willingness to take in "aggressive" dogs who would otherwise be euthanized. On one occasion, she received thirty-two pit bulls from a police raid. Whalen financed the dogs' medical rehabilitation and kept them all—permanently. "I don't adopt out pit bulls," she says. "They would just get abused."

Whalen, like others who run no-kill facilities, is controversial. Some people argue that the quality of life for her dogs and cats is substandard; others line up to give her their pets. Keeping a lid on the population in a no-kill facility is difficult. Whalen has 140 cats. According to one reporter, a shelter in Elmsford, New York, had so many dogs, they were doubled up in cages (a cardinal sin at most shelters) and chained outside. Those were the lucky ones; others were living in hallways and even stashed in the shelter's boiler room.

There are all kinds of shelters and no-kill sanctuaries for dogs, cats, horses, pigs, and just about every other animal. This movement is growing. People leave ample funds in their wills to send their animals to old-age homes where they will live until they die of natural causes. At one such place, cats are welcome for a fee of $3,000; dogs can buy their way in for $5,000. People will pay to keep their animals alive, even if their cats live out their years in cages and their dogs are confined to kennels. Some sanctuaries offer more space, others less. A few allow packs of dogs to run free on vast expanses of fenced-in land, as if they were returning to the wild. Every facility has a slightly different philosophy about what animals need.

Sanctuaries are run by the pro-lifers of the animal welfare movement, which is polarized over euthanasia, in the same way people are divided over the Dr. Kevorkians of the world. But at this point, given the public's indifference to the pet overpopulation crisis, it's hard to imagine what might happen to the animals if euthanasia were forbidden. All shelters, whatever their particular agendas, are already taking in more animals, especially cats, than they can comfortably handle. If every shelter started turning animals away, they would run wild in the streets, spreading disease and breeding indiscriminately, which is what they already do in many third world countries. Some activists believe that the situation *needs* to get really bad before the public will wake up and notice this relatively invisible crisis.

In the meantime, for animal control to be humane and effective, the answer isn't just quietly killing off all the excess pets. Shelters and schools, especially where the students are still dissecting frogs in science class, need to join forces to teach humane education. The laws protecting and emancipating animals have to change. People must be penalized for abandoning, harming, inhumanely slaughtering, or indiscriminately breeding animals for their commercial value.

At this point there is little dialogue between shelters and ordinary pet owners about broader issues like the legal status of animals, backyard breeders, or mandating spaying and neutering for all animals. The shelters themselves are so polarized over the question of euthanasia that the public thinks there are two kinds of shelters: those that kill animals and those that don't. People naturally assume that the latter are more humane. But often this is not the case. The quality of life for animals in no-kill facilities can be just as poor as it is in "full-service" shelters. Shelters that are required to save every animal are generally overrun; many professionals feel that keeping cage-crazy animals is an act of cruelty. Moreover, so-called no-kill shelters often kill; they just don't advertise it.

The quality of life a facility provides for its guests is a critical issue. The finest shelters that I have seen euthanize animals who are suffering or are aggressive quickly and humanely; adoptable animals are only terminated after they are given every chance, with no time limit on how long they can stay. Rescuers and volunteers help place the animals, fostering them when possible to save them from euthanasia. But euthanasia itself will always be an unwelcome, but necessary, element of animal control as long as there are too many animals.

Decent no-kill shelters and private rescuers who do not overload their facilities have a terrible time turning animals away. For them, spaying and neutering every living thing is a religion. Whether a shelter euthanizes or not may be less important than whether a shelter hands out unsterilized animals. Shelters that do hurt the movement and the animals.

"People think we like to euthanize animals," Joan Silaco, a veteran shelter employee, once commented to me. "We have no choice. If we don't do it, someone else is going to. Would that make the public feel better?"

There is a great deal of hypocrisy and willful ignorance on the part of the public around this issue. When surrenderers are told that leaving their unhealthy animals behind will put them immediately at risk for euthanasia, they often leave them anyway. From their point of view, alternative solutions take time and cost money.

"I euthanized twenty-seven animals one evening, including a young black dog," Andrea Walker recalls. "She was very sick with pneumonia. She could have been treated, but the shelter was full and there was no place to keep her warm and isolated. That same evening, I was standing in the cashier line at the grocery store and I saw the couple who had surrendered the dog just ahead of me. I overheard them talking about what kind of dog they were going to buy next! They were discussing Samoyeds versus golden retrievers and planning their trip to the pet store! An hour ago I had held their dog in my arms and taken her life.

"Then the girl's boyfriend noticed me," Andrea continues. "They rushed over, and she said, 'How's Daisy? She's such a good little dog. You'll have no trouble placing her.'" Andrea wanted to strangle them both. Instead, she smiled and said nothing. Then she drove home, lit some candles, and took a long hot bath. This is a ritual Walker devised to help her get to sleep on euthanasia days.

THERE ARE WEEKS when I can't stand to be at Columbia-Greene. I want to scream at every person who comes in to window-shop, kill an afternoon with the kids, and then waltz out empty-handed. For them, there's always something wrong with the pets in stock: they're too big or too small, too ugly, or too old. About 15 percent of the dogs and cats currently in people's homes are adopted from shelters. People want new pets, not secondhand ones. Animal rights advocates, on the other hand, don't think that people should be allowed to keep pets—at all. Ingrid Newkirk, the cofounder of PETA, has said, "You don't have to own squirrels and starlings to get enjoyment from them."

Hostilities between shelter employees and the public tend to be mutual and unremitting. It's a vicious circle. Shelter employees are fed up with people who dump their animals with no remorse, and people resent shelters for euthanizing animals or being self-righteous about who gets to take them home. It's an impossible, almost schizophrenic situation. Shelter workers themselves spend half their time protecting animals and the other half killing them.

The antagonism between shelters and the public is understandable but dangerous. Shelters have to do a much better job reaching out to their communities. They have to become more than animal adoption agencies and abortion or sterilization clinics. They have to become centers of humane education—schools, if you will—teaching a broad curriculum of animal issues.

My own views on the social relations between animals and people swing back and forth as I try to maintain some perspective. It is obvious that pet shops and breeders are a big piece of the problem. The law views companion animals as property, objects to be bought and sold, in part because this is an accurate reflection of how people think about pets. As time goes by, I begin to understand that as long as people can make money off of animals, things will never change. There's a pet industry driving an economy that is based on our insatiable desire for unconditional love.

If, as recently as a hundred years ago, animals were hardworking members of the household, especially on farms, today dogs and cats are superfluous. A few are trained in speciality services, such as leading the blind, sniffing out drugs at airports, or searching for survivors of natural disasters. But the majority of pets are discretionary items, companions for leisure time, or icons to keep chained on the front lawn. They exist only for our pleasure. Once they stop generating pleasure, they are discarded. The public wants them to just disappear.

It is difficult to get a fix on the scandalous treatment of animals in a culture so dedicated to feel-good fantasies and wildly idealized fairy tales about our relations to pets. An elaborate consumer market is built on the upbeat notion that if we pamper our pets, they will be delighted to return our favors. We can buy them gourmet foods; leash systems that don't choke; jeweled collars; toys geared to every stage of animal development; and a range of novelty items, including bad-breath biscuits and specially designed bowls for dogs with long ears, short necks, or unusual heights. There are homeopathic veterinarians, animal masseuses, acupuncturists who are trained to work on horses, and a variety of therapists to eliminate all kinds of irritating habits.

Pet ownership opens up new social arenas, as people meet through dog runs, clubs, rescue organizations, schools, shows, and even shelters where they volunteer. For singles in search of a mate, forget dating services and the personals. As my brother recently explained to me, "Want to meet a girl? Get a puppy."

There is more pet chatting on the Internet than talk about child rearing. People spend hours comparing notes on breeds, idiosyncratic behavioral problems, or the latest exotic pet to bring home. One night, chinchilla fans schedule an on-line meeting; emu farmers meet the next. Homeless animals can find new owners through interactive web sites set up by shelters, breeders, and rescuers. And animal lovers can discuss their pets with the experts—veterinarians, cruelty investigators, breeders, or trainers—or just eavesdrop on their conversations with one another.

The current obsession with animals saturates the media, especially the advertising industry. Animals shamelessly beckon us to buy clothes, cars, Rollerblades, cigarettes, gas, or a trip to the Bahamas, just as nakedly as women used to, prior to our liberation movement. (Women are still out there, but we're not alone, and we know where we stand.) There is every reason to assume that animals are happily integrated into the fabric of our lives.

In a society in which it is difficult for people to recognize that there are human beings who need help, how can they be convinced that animals need help? On the other hand, many people find it easier to sympathize with animals than people. It's as if there are two worlds of animal owners. There are those who obsessively pamper their pets and those who torture theirs. These two groups are not divided neatly by class or financial power. Lori Beckers likes to distinguish between "poor people" and "trash." The former feed their animals first and themselves second. The latter, which includes even the wealthiest owners, allow their pets to starve to death when their cupboards are full.

When Jennifer and Paolo Gucci (of the Italian fashion family) were getting divorced, their Arabian horse farm in Columbia County suffered the consequences. Paolo stopped supporting the horses as well as his wife. Jennifer ultimately had to bring in the Humane Society to monitor the animals' care.

It can be expensive to keep animals, but lack of money isn't the primary reason that people give up their dogs and cats. It's because they put such a low valuation on animals. If all the folks in

Columbia County who told the shelter that they were moving actually moved, the area would be deserted. There are legitimate reasons to give up pets, but the pervasive attitude that they are disposable, like paper cups, has to change. Every time a family surrenders a pet, children are taught that living beings do not have any inherent value.

One fall afternoon, a man with two children, both under ten, walks into the shelter. "Do you take rabbits?" he asks me. "Yes, we do," I tell him. "What's the problem?" He explains that he lives in a New York City apartment and his rabbit is defecating on the terrace. While this doesn't particularly bother his family, his neighbor is having a fit about the odors wafting through his window. Originally, he purchased two rabbits, a male and female, from a pet store around the corner from the shelter, near their weekend home.

As he fills out a surrender sheet for Kirby, I notice that this rabbit has been living on Fifth Avenue. He's probably been nibbling sweet baby greens and gourmet scraps. I ask the man if he still has the female rabbit. He explains that when Kirby began humping her nonstop, they got him fixed by Dr. Susan Tanner, one of the few veterinarians in Columbia County who will neuter rabbits. But much to their annoyance, the humping continued, so they returned the female to the pet store. "I tried to return Kirby, but the store refused to take him back. But we still had a neighbor problem," he explains.

Wondering if he knows that rabbits can be litter-box trained just like cats, I ask the obvious, "Why don't you just keep the rabbit off the terrace?"

"Look," he says, "I told the kids that either they start cleaning up after Kirby or he goes. I'm fed up with it. They didn't take care of him. So that's it."

The man is blaming this small tragedy on his children. But who bought the rabbits anyway? Isn't he responsible for their welfare, too? Children make many promises they don't keep. (My own favorite is the one about cleaning their rooms.) Why would any parent assume that a child can take full responsibility for a pet? The lesson this father wants to teach his kids is that he is a man of his word. But from the Humane Society's point of view, the lesson they have learned, probably for life, is that pets can be rejected when they become inconvenient.

The rabbit went on to a more appreciative home where he was litter-box trained. Kirby is presently running free (inside) with several other rabbits and cats.

During periods when there is an ebb in the flow of animals at the shelter, I remember why these places need to exist. I also remember why we need animals in our lives. From my side of the counter, I get glimpses into the lives of those who have lost their jobs, their families, their homes, their health, and now their loyal companions. Their pets were often all they had left. For them, making the decision to bring their dog or cat to the shelter is the end of the line. Without animals, many people are truly alone. They will have no warm creature to come home to at the end of a long day to make their lives a little bit brighter or, for some, worth living at all.

An older woman, at least seventy-five, wearing an elegant straw hat, walks in lugging a cat carrier, a tall scratching post, and a bag of food. The woman radiates a genuine warmth. I can see her in church on Sundays with her relatives, or bending over to take an apple pie out of the oven. But something is very wrong. The woman is all alone and visibly nervous and upset. She explains that she has lived in Hudson all her life and her children are scattered all over the country. After more than fifty years in the same home, she has just been robbed. Everything she had left of any value has been taken. She doesn't know what she's going to do or where she's going to end up living. The future terrifies her. Now the little black-and-white kitten she just took in is a problem. She wants the kitten to have a better life than she can offer. "She's so young," the woman tells Sylvia Lehtinen, a new adoption counselor, as she begins to weep. "Can you find her a home while she still has a chance to grow up feeling loved?"

"Of course we will," Sylvia responds, starting to weep right along with her. "Don't you worry." Now Sylvia will do the worrying for her. She will figure out how to present this kitten to the public so that they will want to open up her cage and lift her into their arms. Maybe the kitten's picture will get into the paper; maybe she can go out to a pet fair and connect with a passerby. Her name is Eve, and as it turns out, she goes home.

Alexis, a rescued pit bull, is now a
working therapy dog.

Afterword:
Finding the Right Pet

I T' S N O S E C R E T that we get pets to improve the quality of our
own lives. But for animals to make a difference, they must be
treated with respect. People who were raised with pets, including
dogs and cats, frequently assume that they require very little care.
This is an illusion. When you were little, having pets was a breeze
because your parents did all the work. Taking good care of a pet,
whether it is a tiny tetra or a large Thoroughbred, requires a significant investment in time and money. Even tropical fish are far
from maintenance free; you practically have to become an amateur
ichthyologist to maintain a healthy environment in a tank.

Animals need time to adjust to their new homes. Younger pets
require more attention for their first few years until they learn to

live within the parameters of their new lifestyle. Most dogs, for instance, will bond quickly with their owners, but when they are first left alone, they can develop nervous habits that will plague them (and you) for years. Cats are more independent by nature, but they, too, need time to accept the boundaries of their new habitats. The reason there are so many young animals in shelters is that people get impatient and give up before their pets have time to integrate themselves into their owners' lives. These are people who probably shouldn't have had pets to begin with.

Make sure you are getting a pet for the right reasons. Any child who goes to the movies and watches television quite naturally wants a pet and tons of candy. You can limit the candy. But once you bring a puppy home, the animal's needs won't wane even if your child's interest does. If your children want a dog, but you don't—*don't get one.* You will begrudge the amount of work involved in exercising, feeding, training, grooming, and vetting a dog if he or she was acquired simply to entertain the kids. Young children require even more supervision when there are pets around. And when you go on vacation, someone still has to feed the animals.

If it's the appropriate moment for you to get a pet, I hope your first step will be to find your local shelter. Given the variety of animals available in most facilities, your chances of finding the right dog or cat are excellent. If you assume that the "best" animals in shelters are skimmed off the top and taken home by employees and insiders, you are absolutely wrong. At Columbia-Greene, staffers go for the most unadoptable animals to save them from euthanasia. The youngest, healthiest, cutest pets are waiting for you.

Some people avoid shelters because of their reputations for

rigorous adoption procedures. I have never come across an application form that couldn't be filled out in fifteen minutes. If you have read this book, then you know that there are good reasons for these policies. A strict adoption protocol is frequently an indication of a quality shelter. If you were surrendering an animal, instead of adopting one, wouldn't you want your pet placed as carefully as possible?

Before you visit any shelter, you need to make a few decisions based on your living situation. Do you reside in the country or the city? In an apartment or a house? Are there children? Most families are looking for purebred pets who look like movie stars. Before you even think about breeds, consider whether you want a young or an adult animal. Don't assume that you *have* to get a puppy or a kitten because they are so adorable or that older animals come with too much baggage. It's just not true. Older animals are often already trained, more mellow, and generally more responsive to people. They are frequently better with children. Puppies treat kids like their own littermates; they mouth them constantly—with razor-sharp teeth.

Of course, if you decide on a puppy, you must make time for some training. First, read some books *before* you bring home the dog. (First-time pet owners should read Carol Lea Benjamin's *Second-Hand Dog* or *The Chosen Puppy*. Also popular are *The Art of Raising a Puppy* and *How to Be Your Dog's Best Friend* by the Monks of New Skate.) Joining a basic obedience-training class is the fastest and most effective way to train any dog. The myth that older dogs can't be taught anything new is completely unfounded. Dogs of all ages thrive in classes where they get to be with their own kind and work for treats. There are many levels of training, and people often keep working with their dogs for years. It's fun. Training is also an ideal way to bond with your new pet.

Decide how much time you really want to put into a dog. How many hours a day are you away from home? Be realistic—everybody works for a living. If you are away from home all day, you might want a dog who is already housebroken and partially trained. Ask a shelter employee which dogs can be left alone for long periods of time without wreaking havoc. You will have some brief transition problems when you take these dogs home, but they will settle down much faster than puppies.

These decisions will weed out certain animals, making the selection process easier. You may even conclude that you need a cat in your life rather than a dog. Cats value their time alone. They have different needs.

Educate yourself about breeds. Dogs and cats have been bred for centuries to have specific characteristics or traits, which will manifest themselves to different degrees, despite the mixed ancestry of crossbreeds. Don't be guided by the all-too-prevalent myths about dogs: pit bulls are not inherently vicious (although some of their owners might be); greyhounds are not born to run. Indeed, pit bulls are not for everyone, but they are extremely intelligent and loyal, while greyhounds are couch potatoes and make ideal pets. If you live in the country, you might consider a herding breed, otherwise your Border collie, cattle dog, or Australian shepherd might start nipping at the heels of joggers in the park.

If you are a person who knows dogs and you have your heart set on a Saluki or a borzoi (two breeds among many that are unusual to find in a shelter), call their rescue groups. (They can usually be contacted through the Internet or your local shelter.) If you want a puppy and none are available, you either have to put your name on a list or consider going to a breeder.

My friend Ernie, who loves his basset hound, Sugar Ray, as if he were his son, recently asked me if I thought it was immoral to get a dog from a breeder. Not exactly. I think it is immoral for breeders to breed dogs like chickens and send them off through the mail or in substandard vehicles to pet stores. The problem is that most breeders produce more dogs than they can sell either out of their homes or to pet stores. They frequently keep dozens of dogs who live out their lives in small cages. When breeding is motivated by profit, animals suffer.

There are also far too many individual dog owners who breed their pets out of a combination of love and ignorance. They do not know what's in the bloodline, how to pick a proper mate for their dog, or the procedures for carefully placing the offspring. These are the folks who put their ads in the paper when they can't get rid of the puppies by word of mouth. Obviously there are some quality humane breeders around who do not produce an over abundance of litters. Why would they, when there are millions of unwanted animals in shelters?

Most people just want affectionate pets, and for that, mixed breeds are every bit as good—sometimes better—than purebreds. Mixed breeds also come in all sizes, colors, shapes, and ages. There is no reason automatically to go to a breeder when shelters are euthanizing perfectly good pets.

People stay away from shelters because they assume they are dirty and noisy. But Columbia-Greene, for instance, is cleaner than many pet stores I have visited in New York City. Nevertheless, shelters house more animals than stores, and the environment in the kennels is geared to the animals, not the shopper. There is no reason for a shelter to stink unless the kennel workers are not doing their job. But you must prepare yourself for the noise. Shelter dogs tend to bark constantly, largely to keep from going crazy with boredom. If one barks, usually they all go off. Don't penalize them for acting like dogs.

Selecting an animal from a shelter can actually be an educational experience. If they can, staff members will spend time with adopters, discussing the pluses and minuses of individual animals, their breeds, and histories. People have specific needs from animals and often attach sentimental value to breeds. Some people like Labs better than retrievers or have a special fondness for hounds. For others, selecting a dog that doesn't shed (usually anything with poodle or terrier in the mix) is the goal.

People are frequently searching for watchdogs, but virtually any dog, once it is part of a family, will become protective; they almost all bark when strangers show up. Still, submissives will lick an intruder to death rather than go for the jugular. If you really want to make sure your jewels are safe, go for a dominant breed like a shepherd, Doberman, or rottweiler. It's not that these dogs are aggressive but that burglars will incorrectly assume they are. Bear in mind that owning a dominant breed dog may drive up your liability insurance. These dogs also need consistent training.

Many families are just looking for a pooch who will be good with children. If you have kids under ten, ask the shelter for a list of available dogs who are child-friendly. Dominant breeds, as well as dalmatians, cocker spaniels, and small terriers, tend to prefer adults unless they have been successfully raised with kids.

What size pet should you get? If you live in a small city apartment with no open space to run a dog, don't bring home a Saint Bernard or any dog who needs a great deal of exercise. All dogs need some exercise, but smaller breeds require less space to do it in. If you live in a five-story walk-up, forget about basset hounds or any heavy dog with very short legs; they have enough trouble scooting along on flat surfaces.

In every shelter, you will meet animals who show signs of having been abused. Typically, these dogs are withdrawn and hand-shy; that is, they dash away or duck when you reach out to them. Some need extra coaxing before they will even approach you, but these are often minor behavioral problems that can be corrected. As soon as the animals are convinced that you won't hurt them, they will begin to trust you. Other problems are shelter-specific. Stress, changes in diet, or even the chemicals used to clean the kennels can cause rashes, hair loss, or hyperactivity. It's always a good idea to consult the experts—vets and trainers—but all these conditions should disappear when the animal leaves the shelter. Sometimes the dogs who are most stressed out are the most relaxed once they are out of the pound.

Before you walk through the kennel, encourage the staff to suggest particular animals whom they think you might want. Often, people come to find a particular kind of dog or cat but end up falling in love with a completely different type because the staff pointed them in a new direction. People who lose their pets come through shelters hoping to find one who looks exactly the same as their old one. Sometimes they find such an animal, but frequently they are motivated by grief and are not really ready for a new pet. Find out what services the shelter offers; grief counseling can make a difference when that inevitable day comes and your pet dies.

Never judge an animal in a cage. Both cats and dogs are different behind bars and infinitely more congenial once they are free. Take the dog for a walk, preferably outside, before making a final decision. Shelter dogs have a tendency to be hyper and excited by visitors. They may jump all over you, but that doesn't necessarily mean that the dog has a frantic disposition. Give the dog some exercise. A walk will tire the dog out a little, which will help him or her to relax. Afterward find somewhere to rest, and try to get the dog to sit and calm down. If the dog is distracted and won't settle—don't worry. The dog lives in a cage and is already starting to worry about when you are going to put him or her back into it.

The more time you spend with an animal, the more that animal will begin to respond to you. Be patient. Try to get the dog to look you in the eye; talk to the dog and massage him or her behind the ears and on the back (they love to be rubbed). If you have time, ask the shelter for a brush and do some grooming; this is a great way to get to know an animal. Some dogs will bond with you immediately, while others need more reassurance. Dogs do not forget people. Come back and visit a second time, and the dog should be noticeably more responsive. Once they get home and begin to feel safe, they really start to unwind.

Some shelters have small visitation rooms where adopters can get to know the cats. Never grab a cat or chase after one; let the cat come to you. I have seen the most hissy felines turn into affectionate creatures once they are allowed some independence. Cats can be leery of strangers. Many have also gone through rough stray periods prior to ending up in shelters. Some want to be handled and will purr with happiness the minute they are held, but others are more standoffish. Some people prefer independent personalities; others want cuddlers.

Shelters have purebred and mixed breed cats, although most staffers are not trained to identify them. Do some research. Cats, like dogs, have different characteristics and needs based on their genetics. Siamese can be constant talkers; Persians may need to have their faces washed. Some longhairs require grooming, while many can do this job for themselves.

If you have a declawed cat at home, ask the shelter if there are others available. Bringing home a cat with nails puts your declawed one at risk. (Don't let declawed cats outside; most of them can't get up trees to escape predators.) Some shelters reject adopters who intend to surgically remove a cat's nails; certain veterinarians also consider the operation to be inhumane. People don't realize that they can clip a cat's nails with their own personal clippers—not too short, however, or you will draw blood. Cats usually don't appreciate this process, but they can be trained to accept it as part of their routine. There shouldn't be any need to declaw if you get a good scratching post and rub catnip all over it. Moreover, declawed cats often start to bite. Their teeth are their only weapons.

Shelters have all kinds of cats, with or without nails. If you have no other pet at home, consider adopting two cats; they are happiest with company and endlessly entertaining when they play. Also, contrary to conventional wisdom, dogs and cats do not detest one another: they often get along quite well. Tibbs, my cat, is nuts about Tramp, and they play together constantly. (Snowy, however, is indifferent to the species.)

Find out what vaccines the shelter has given the animals. If you have other cats at home, you don't want to bring one in with feline leukemia. Expect minor health problems that might have been overlooked when you first take home a cat or a dog. There is no reason not to adopt an animal with a treatable illness, like a cold. Many shelters will send animals home with appropriate medications.

Get as much information from the shelter as possible about the history of the cat or dog whom you want to adopt. If none is available (largely because the shelter screwed up and failed to get adequate information from the previous owner), ask if it is possible for anyone to make further inquiries. Employees may consider this request to be beyond the call of duty. If you're lucky, someone will take the time to make a phone call and get some information. (Shelters will not—and should not—give out a surrenderer's name to an adopter.) If the animal came in stray, talk directly to the kennel workers who have been caring for him or her. They frequently know the cats and dogs more intimately than the adoption counselors do. Don't be leery of strays. They often turn out to be the most even-tempered animals in residence.

People do not realize that all kinds of animals, apart from cats and dogs, are also available at shelters. It is common to find birds, snakes, ferrets, pigs, and a variety of rodents, including mice, rats, guinea pigs, and hamsters. In rural areas, homes for horses, cows, sheep, chickens, and goats are needed. In New York City's shelter, I have met monkeys, squirrels, seagulls, turtles, and iguanas. Let your local shelter know if you can offer a home to one of the more unusual pets. Many facilities keep lists of people who are looking for specific creatures. When the phone rings, and it is a shelter employee calling about that parrot you've been waiting for, or maybe the mature papillon, it is thrilling to answer, "I'll be right over."

If your local shelter is less than an ideal place for animals—*go there anyway.* Many impoverished facilities are staffed with minimum wage employees who work hard but have little interest in animals. Remind yourself that the animals are not responsible for their predicament. Moreover, they are counting on you to find them and take them home.

Index